ATIVIDADES DE VÍDEO PARA O ENSINO DE INGLÊS

ATIVIDADES DE VÍDEO

PARA O ENSINO DE INGLÊS

Louise Emma Potter
Ligia Lederman

Louise Potter atua na área de ensino de Língua Estrangeira e treinamento de professores há mais de 20 anos, tendo como áreas de especialização *teacher trainning* e *teacher development*. Comandou equipes de professores por 12 anos em escola de idiomas e é autora de materiais didáticos para língua inglesa. É sócia proprietária da Teach-in Education, empresa de capacitação e treinamento para professores de Língua Estrangeira.

Ligia Lederman é especialista em Linguística Aplicada ao Ensino de Língua Estrangeira pela Unicamp, professora e autora de materiais didáticos de inglês, diretora e orientadora pedagógica de escola de idiomas.

Capa e projeto gráfico: Città Estúdio
Editoração eletrônica: Città Estúdio
Supervisão Editorial: Faccioli Editorial
Revisão: Sandra Garcia Cortés

Dados Internacionais de Catalogação na Publicação (CIP)
(Câmara Brasileira do Livro, SP, Brasil)

Potter, Louise Emma
Atividade de vídeo : para o ensino de inglês / Louise Emma Potter, Ligia Lederman. -- Barueri, SP : DISAL, 2012. -- (Coleção estratégias)

Bibliografia
ISBN 978-85-7844-098-5

1. Atividades de vídeo 2. Ensino - Materiais didáticos 3. Inglês - Atividades, exercícios etc. 4. Inglês - Estudo e ensino I. Lederman, Ligia. II. Título. III. Série.

12-00398 CDD-420.7

Índices para catálogo sistemático:

1. Atividades de vídeo : Inglês : Estudo e ensino 420.7

DISAL EDITORA

Bantim, Canato e Guazzelli Editora Ltda.
Alameda Mamoré 911 – cj. 107
Alphaville – BARUERI – SP
CEP: 06454-040
Tel. / Fax: (11) 4195-2811
Visite nosso site: www.disaleditora.com.br
Televendas: (11) 3226-3111
Fax gratuito: 0800 7707 105/106
E-mail para pedidos: comercial@disal.com.br

Impressão e acabamento: Yangraf Gráfica e Editora

CITAÇÕES DE FILMES

It takes a great deal of bravery to stand up to your enemies, but a great deal more to stand up to your friends.
Dumbledore, from *Harry Potter and the Philosopher's Stone*

You can't lose something you never had!
Andie Anderson, from *How to Lose a Guy in Ten Days*

That's what people do. They leap, and hope to God they can fly...
Alex Hitchens, from *Hitch*

I just need to know that it's possible that two people can stay happy together forever.
Juno MacGuff, from *Juno*

Never lie, steal, cheat, or drink. But if you must lie, lie in the arms of the one you love. If you must steal, steal away from bad company. If you must cheat, cheat death. And if you must drink, drink in the moments that take your breath away.
Alex Hitchens, from ***Hitch***

Fear can hold you prisoner. Hope can set you free.
Red, from *The Shawshank Redemption*

SUMÁRIO

INTRODUÇÃO

No mundo globalizado de hoje temos acesso cada vez maior a uma gama de informações vindas de todos os meios de comunicação: jornais, revistas, internet, cinema, televisão, jogos interativos etc. Percebemos que cada vez mais a língua inglesa está presente nesses meios e, assim, cria-se a necessidade de expor os alunos a diferentes oportunidades de interagir e organizar essas informações recebidas. A sala de aula de Língua Estrangeira (LE) mudou. Precisamos ir além do ensino das estruturas gramaticais não contextualizadas. Devemos envolver nossos alunos e expô-los a diferentes gêneros que estão presentes no seu cotidiano, trazendo essa realidade para a sala de aula. Como professoras de inglês, percebemos a necessidade de desenvolver meios mais próximos da realidade dos alunos para atingir objetivos linguísticos e pedagógicos e, dessa forma, motivá-los a participar mais ativamente da aula e aprender de maneira mais prazerosa.

O objetivo deste livro é orientar professores de Língua Inglesa a preparar e utilizar atividades de vídeo como atividades complementares à sala de aula.

O livro é dividido em duas partes. Na primeira encontram-se as atividades fotocopiáveis para os alunos. Na segunda, você encontrará sinopses, informações técnicas, dicas para o professor e respostas das atividades.

Há dois grupos de atividades. O primeiro contém 10 trailers com atividades mais curtas (20 minutos) para serem usadas tanto para *warm-ups* no início de uma aula como para revisão de conteúdos. O segundo contém 20 filmes com atividades planejadas para uma aula (50 minutos). As atividades estão divididas por níveis: básico, pré-intermediário, intermediário e avançado.

Antes de cada grupo de atividades, os filmes estão organizados em quadros, para ajudá-lo a escolher a sequência mais adequada para o perfil da sua classe.

Como todo professor sabe, o planejamento é um passo de extrema importância para que o resultado seja positivo. Esperamos que você encontre neste livro ideias para planejar e tornar sua sala de aula um ambiente de interação e aprendizagem de LE mais motivador.

POR QUE USAR VÍDEOS?

Nós, educadores, sabemos como é importante motivar nossos alunos de LE. Os vídeos ativam as emoções dos alunos, criam ambientes diferentes de acordo com o filme, engajam-nos em atividades prazerosas e, acima de tudo, têm um resultado positivo na aprendizagem.

Ao usar vídeos com nossos alunos, fornecemo-lhes diversas perspectivas de um mesmo tema, podemos aproximá-los de diferentes culturas, fazê-los perceber sua própria cultura em comparação à cultura do outro, estimular o pensamento crítico, revisar vocabulário e estruturas gramaticais, expô-los a variados tipos de pronúncia e à linguagem de falantes nativos em um ambiente seguro e ainda expandir sua visão de mundo.

A sala de aula é um ambiente heterogêneo, composto de alunos com estilos de aprendizagem diversos. Um ensino de qualidade atende às necessidades de cada aluno, respeita seu estilo de aprendizagem e lhe dá condições para atingir seu objetivo individual. Com a utilização de vídeos, o professor consegue alcançar de forma mais abrangente essas necessidades individuais.

Por meio dos vídeos, também desenvolvemos as competências comunicativas (Savignon, 1972) dos alunos, que podem ser divididas em:

1. Competência gramatical: implica o domínio do código linguístico, a habilidade em reconhecer as características linguísticas da língua e usá-las para formar palavras e frases;
2. Competência sociolinguística: implica o conhecimento das regras sociais que norteiam o uso da língua e a compreensão do contexto social no qual a língua é usada;
3. Competência discursiva: diz respeito à conexão de uma série de orações e frases com a finalidade de formar um todo significativo. Esse conhecimento tem de ser compartilhado pelo falante/escritor e ouvinte/leitor;
4. Competência estratégica: diz respeito às estratégias que devem ser usadas para compensar qualquer imperfeição no conhecimento das regras.

A preparação e a utilização das atividades de vídeo devem ser realizadas de forma crítica e cuidadosa, para que alcancemos o melhor resultado possível. Para orientá-lo no seu planejamento, explicitamos quais competências são desenvolvidas em cada atividade.

COMO PLANEJAR ATIVIDADES DE VÍDEO

Before the video class

- Existem diversos gêneros de vídeos que podem ser utilizados para preparar as atividades: filmes históricos, biográficos, comédia, romance, ficção, desenhos animados, filmes contemporâneos e ainda os seriados, vídeos do YouTube, clipes etc. É importante conhecer o perfil de seus alunos antes de escolher o vídeo que será utilizado. Converse com eles para descobrir suas preferências e escolha com cuidado. Dessa forma os alunos serão motivados e estimulados a aprender.
- Certifique-se de que haja uma relação entre o conteúdo do vídeo e o objetivo pedagógico do curso em andamento. O tópico que está sendo apresentado em sala de aula deve ter uma relação direta com a atividade de vídeo que você desenvolverá.
- É importante que o vídeo seja apropriado para a faixa etária do seu grupo de alunos. Por exemplo: ao abordar temas polêmicos, certifique-se de que seus alunos têm maturidade para discutir o assunto.
- Escolha um pequeno segmento do vídeo (de 3 a 10 minutos) relacionado ao seu objetivo. É essencial que você escolha cuidadosamente a sequência que será utilizada de acordo com o nível linguístico dos alunos. Os alunos podem ser expostos a uma linguagem mais elaborada, mas a atividade proposta deve ser possível de ser realizada.
- Assista aos vídeos várias vezes e certifique-se de que tenha entendido plenamente todo o vocabulário.
- Prepare atividades variadas que possam ser desenvolvidas durante o período de uma aula. (Lembre-se de que os alunos assistirão ao vídeo mais de uma vez.)
- Confira se o equipamento a ser usado está funcionando e disponível.

During the video class

- Devemos ter o cuidado de enfatizar o **objetivo** que se quer alcançar. Lembre-se de que essas atividades são complementares e proporcionam a oportunidade de rever conceitos gramaticais, lexicais, além de desenvolver competências estratégicas de forma motivadora. Isso deve ser explicitado aos alunos por meio de instruções claras, antes da atividade.
- Ao iniciar a atividade de vídeo, devemos ativar o **conhecimento prévio** dos alunos através de perguntas sobre o tema. Observe como isso é feito nas atividades apresentadas neste livro.

- Devemos utilizar estratégias para desenvolver a **acuidade auditiva** dos alunos, caminhando do mais geral para o mais específico, de maneira gradativa. Por exemplo, ao propor uma atividade, podemos tirar a imagem e concentrar a atenção dos alunos somente na audição, solicitando que tenham como foco os sons de fundo, o número de pessoas que estão falando, o tom da voz, ou seja, tópicos mais gerais. Em seguida, podemos fazer perguntas mais específicas.
- Podemos desenvolver atividades de **vocabulário** com o objetivo de apresentar vocabulário novo e reforçar vocabulário conhecido, além de propor que deduzam o significado de palavras novas pelo contexto apresentado.
- Podemos reforçar o entendimento do uso de **tópicos gramaticais** apresentados em sala de aula. Usamos o contexto para que os reconheçam e em seguida os utilizem.
- Podemos desenvolver atividades de **leitura** utilizando as legendas. Se o objetivo for desenvolver estratégias de leitura, apresente o vídeo sem o som, somente com legendas.
- Devemos expor os alunos às **variedades da língua inglesa** e também às **diferentes culturas** dos países falantes da língua inglesa. Podemos escolher vídeos em que as pessoas sejam de diferentes regiões dos vários países falantes de inglês. Podemos apontar para os usos da língua entre pessoas de diferentes faixas etárias, classes sociais, sexos e etnias.
- Podemos estimular a **criatividade** por meio do uso de **insumos visuais**, apresentando apenas a imagem sem o som. Dessa forma, os alunos têm a oportunidade de levantar hipóteses sobre o tema, levando em consideração somente a imagem. Por exemplo, ao mostrar uma imagem de uma família conversando, podemos perguntar aos alunos quem são aquelas pessoas, que tipo de relacionamento existe entre elas, quais assuntos estão sendo discutidos etc. Podemos também pedir aos alunos que criem um diálogo com base na cena a que assistiram.
- Devemos desenvolver o **senso crítico** dos alunos por meio dos temas polêmicos escolhidos e, ao mesmo tempo, rever e discutir valores.

After the video class

- Devemos fazer perguntas aos alunos para nos certificarmos de que eles entenderam o objetivo e de que este foi realmente alcançado.
- Devemos propor atividades extraclasse de acordo com o objetivo linguístico escolhido. Por exemplo, uma atividade escrita, assistir ao filme todo em casa e trazer informações novas para a aula seguinte; ler o livro correspondente etc.

COMO CONDUZIR UMA AULA DE VÍDEO

BEFORE VIEWING

Escolha até dois dos tópicos abaixo:

> Estimule o **conhecimento prévio** do aluno fazendo perguntas relevantes a respeito do tópico.

> Elabore o **levantamento de hipóteses** a respeito do **título** do vídeo. Podem-se levantar hipóteses a respeito do **tópico** escrevendo algumas palavras-chave na lousa e pedindo que os alunos imaginem qual tema será abordado.

> Peça que os alunos façam **anotações** sobre o que eles já sabem a respeito do tópico, para utilizá-las após assistir ao vídeo.

> Organize os alunos em pequenos grupos e peça que cada grupo faça um **resumo** sobre o que os integrantes sabem a respeito do tópico. Solicite que façam um levantamento de **dúvidas** que possam ter sobre o tema. Eles devem responder a essas dúvidas após assistir ao vídeo.

VIEWING

Dê aos alunos tarefas com objetivos específicos:

> Busca de expressões do dia a dia. Escolha no vídeo algumas sentenças que possam ser úteis para seus alunos e peça que eles as encontrem. Por exemplo: *How are you doing?*, *Watch out for the step!*, *Over here!*, *It's been great seeing you!*, *Don't make things difficult!*, *How does he look?* etc.

> Reconhecimento ou expansão de vocabulário: busca de objetos que podem ser vistos no vídeo; *brainstorm* de palavras que podem aparecer no vídeo etc.

> Reforço de estruturas gramaticais: reconhecimento dos tempos verbais e seu uso; emprego de preposições por meio de perguntas: *Where is the hairbrush? It is* on *the sink.*

> Reconhecimento do uso de funções tais como: convite, recusa, pedido em restaurante, conversa ao telefone, apresentações, *small talk*, descrição de locais etc. Uma atividade relacionada a essas funções pode ser elaborada em seguida.

> Elaboração de questões de múltipla escolha ou perguntas e respostas.

> Elaboração de perguntas pelo professor com base na sequência assistida. O aluno pode formular uma pergunta para que o colega responda.

- Elaboração de respostas de acordo com a sequência assistida para que o aluno formule a pergunta correspondente.
- Ordenação de sentenças ou palavras de acordo com os diálogos do vídeo.
- Utilização do vídeo como *input* para a escrita: os alunos devem escrever um roteiro ou diálogos relacionados com o tema, fazer um resumo depois de assistir à sequência de vídeo e podem ainda criar um diálogo baseado em uma cena sem som.
- Utilização do vídeo como *input* para leitura: os alunos podem ler o livro depois de assistir ao filme.
- Registro por escrito de fatos interessantes ou informações pessoais.
- Atividades de completar sentenças.
- Criação de diálogos.
- Atividades de relacionar colunas.
- Compreensão auditiva.
- Verdadeiro ou Falso.
- Classificação, organização e ordenação.
- Utilização do vídeo sem a imagem. Cubra a tela com papel e peça aos alunos que ouçam e façam um levantamento de informações antes de assistirem. Quais os papéis da música e da narração? Solicite que criem suas próprias imagens e, em seguida, as comparem com as imagens do vídeo.
- Assistir ao vídeo sem som. Peça aos alunos que criem um diálogo correspondente à cena a que assistiram.
- Uso da legenda como uma atividade de leitura, com ou sem som.

AFTER VIEWING

- Peça aos alunos que releiam as anotações que fizeram no *Before viewing* e comparem com o que descobriram a partir do vídeo.
- Solicite aos grupos que respondam às perguntas feitas no *Before viewing* e discutam as informações adquiridas.
- Organize os alunos em pares e peça-lhes que troquem informações a respeito do vídeo.
- Peça aos alunos que escrevam um pequeno texto a respeito do vídeo, relatando suas impressões pessoais.
- Escolha quatro tópicos referentes ao vídeo e coloque-os em uma folha de papel em cada canto da sala. Peça aos alunos que escolham o canto que esteja relacionado com o tópico que eles queiram explorar. Prepare uma atividade diferente sobre cada tópico e peça-lhes que troquem ideias e as reportem para a classe. Os alunos também podem passar pelos quatro cantos da sala e fazer todas as atividades, se houver tempo.

ATIVIDADES DE

VÍDEO

PARTE 1: *TRAILERS*

Atividades de 20 minutos

TITLE	CONTEXT	LEVEL
1. The Tourist [O Turista]	Transportation Adverbs of frequency	Basic
2. Oceans [Oceanos]	Sea animals and Earth Day	Basic
3. Friends – Season 4 – Episode 4 – The One with the Ballroom Dancing – At the Gym	Sports, quitting activities and giving opinions	Basic
4. Rio	Endangered species	Basic
5. The Social Network [A Rede Social]	Social networks	Pre-intermediate
6. Philadelphia [Filadélfia]	Discriminations	Pre-intermediate
7. Avatar	Life on other planets	Intermediate
8. The King's Speech [O Discurso do Rei]	Giving presentations	Intermediate
9. Desert Flower [Flor do Deserto]	Changing your destiny	Intermediate
10. The Samurai (part 1/10)	Different Cultures, Japan and Samurais	Intermediate and Advanced

THE TOURIST

(O TURISTA)

Disponível em: <http://www.youtube.com/watch?v=GrqpKEOF8uw&feature=related>. Acesso em: 22/09/2011.

BEFORE VIEWING

1. Do you like visiting places?
2. What kind of places do you like visiting?
3. What kind of transportation do you usually use on your trips?
4. Which is your favorite?
5. Are you afraid of using any kind of transportation? Why?

VIEWING

I. Answer the following questions after watching the trailer.

1. What are the actor's and actress' real names?

____

2. What are their names in the film?

____

3. What kind of movie do you think it is?

____

4. Where do the characters meet?

____

5. Where does the story take place?

____

6. What kind of transportation can you see in the trailer?

____

7. How does the woman introduce the man at the hotel?

____

II. Complete the dialogue that Frank has on the phone with the hotel receptionist.

Frank: Hello. _______________ There are two men trying to break down _______________.

Receptionist: _______________ of problem do you have with the door, sir?

Frank: No, no, there are two men with guns trying to break in. I've got to go.

III. What are the meanings of these expressions?

1. Break down ______________________________

2. Break into ______________________________

IV. Make up two sentences using the expressions above.

____

____

AFTER VIEWING

I. Classify the following words in the columns below.

speed boat airplane scooter gondola bike car
helicopter ship hovercraft subway train truck
motorbike zeppelin hot air balloon bus

IN THE AIR	IN THE WATER	ON THE ROAD

II. In pairs, tell your friend how often you do these actions.

Use: Always, never, rarely, sometimes or usually

to catch a bus
to get on a bus
to get off a bus
to drive a car
to ride a bike
to fly a plane/helicopter
to take a boat

OCEANS

(OCEANOS)

Disponível em: <http://www.youtube.com/watch?v=ARFH4aXYFFM>. Acesso em: 22/09/2011.

BEFORE VIEWING

1. When is Earth Day?
2. What do you know about it? What do we celebrate?
3. Are oceans important for the Earth?
4. Do you think we, human beings, know a lot about the oceans?
5. Do you know how much of our planet consists of water?
6. Do you know any sea animals? Can you name them?

VIEWING

1. Watch the trailer and check the animals you see.

☐ sharks	☐ whales	☐ fish	☐ turtles
☐ jelly fish	☐ seagulls	☐ dolphins	☐ ray
☐ starfish	☐ shrimp	☐ squid	☐ seal
☐ walrus	☐ octopus	☐ pelican	☐ lobster
☐ seahorse	☐ school of fish	☐ iguanas	☐ penguins

2. How much have we seen of the oceans according to Silvia, the oceanographer?

____

AFTER VIEWING

1. What can we do to protect our environment?

____

____

____

2. What do you already do to protect our environment?

____

____

____

____

____

____

____

THE ONE WITH THE BALLROOM DANCING – AT THE GYM

Disponível em: <http://www.youtube.com/watch?v=C_ESeEZD_0Y>. Acesso em: 27/09/2011.

BEFORE VIEWING

1. Do you like sports? What kind of sports do you like?
2. Do you like going to the gym?
3. If yes, how often do you go?
4. Do you practice any other sports besides going to the gym?
5. Have you ever quit any sports you started? Why?

VIEWING

Mark True or False.

1. ☐ Chandler and Ross are members of the gym.
2. ☐ The gym is the worst equipped gym in New York.
3. ☐ Chandler thinks it's easy to quit the gym.
4. ☐ Ross doesn't want to join the gym.
5. ☐ Ross is easily influenced to become a member of the gym.

AFTER VIEWING

1. Are you a quitter?

____

____

____

2. What important things have you quit in your life?

____

____

____

3. Is there a right moment to quit things?

____

____

____

RIO

Disponível em: <http://www.youtube.com/watch?v=P1GRO31ve5Q&NR=1>. Acesso em: 28/09/2011.

BEFORE VIEWING

1. Can you give three examples of endangered species?
2. Do you know the reasons why these animals are becoming extinct?
3. How can we help protect them? Is there anything we can do?

VIEWING

I. Answer the following questions after watching the video.

1. What's Blu's problem?
2. Where does he live?
3. Where does he go?
4. How can you tell that?
5. Who does he meet there?

II. Organize the sequence of events.

- [ ] Blu and Jewel fall on the beach.
- [ ] Blu brushes his teeth.
- [ ] Blu meets Jewel.
- [ ] Blu goes to Rio.
- [ ] Blu and Jewel fall on a hang glider.
- [ ] Blu and Jewel escape from the cage.

III. Match the characters.

1. Blu	( ) the American girl
2. Jewel	( ) the male macaw
3. Linda	( ) the female macaw
4. Tulio	( ) the dog
5. Rafael	( ) the Brazilian guy
6. Luiz	( ) the toucan

IV. Match the characters to the sentences.

1. Good morning, Blu.	( ) Tulio
2. I'm going to make you look irresistible!	( ) Linda
3. I think they need a little help!	( ) Blu
4. I have nothing to do with that!	( ) Blu
5. Hey, what are you doing?	( ) Luiz
6. Getting out of here.	( ) Jewel
7. Is there anything else I need to know?	( ) Jewel
8. This is the most beautiful thing I've ever seen.	( ) Blu
9. All right, Blu. You're flying!	( ) Rafael
10. Don't worry. He's a professional.	( ) Tulio

THE SOCIAL NETWORK

(A REDE SOCIAL)

Disponível em: <http://www.youtube.com/watch?v=lB95KLmpLR4>. Acesso em: 28/09/2011.

BEFORE VIEWING

1. What are your feelings towards social networks?
2. What are their functions?
3. What are the pros and cons of being part of a social network?
4. Which social networks do you know?
5. Which ones do you use?
6. Do you know how Facebook started?

VIEWING

Order the sentences.

☐ Thousand... Twenty-two thousand.

☐ People want to go on the internet and check out their friends so why not build a website that offers that. Friends, pictures, profiles... I am talking about taking the entire social experience of college and putting it online.

☐ Millions?

☐ I need to do something substantial in order to get the attention of the clubs.

☐ This idea is potentially worth millions of dollars.

☐ Why?

☐ You got twenty-two hundred hits within two hours?

☐ You stole our website.

☐ Because they are exclusive and fun and lead to a better life.

AFTER VIEWING

1. What else do you do on the internet?

____

____

____

2. Do you believe fame can spoil your relationships?

____

____

3. What is more important: to be professionally successful or to have a stable relationship?

____

____

____

PHILADELPHIA

(FILADÉLFIA)

Disponível em: <http://www.youtube.com/watch?v=cl4B9AU45P4>.
Acesso em: 28/09/2011.

BEFORE VIEWING

1. What does discrimination mean to you?
2. Mention different ways people can discriminate people.
3. Do you believe one can discriminate a person for having a non-contagious disease?

VIEWING

1. What kind of company do you think Andrew works for?

___

___

2. "I sincerely appreciate your faith in my abilities". Who said this? What were the circumstances?

___

___

3. What disease does Andrew have?

___

___

4. How long ago was Andrew diagnosed with this disease?

___

___

5. Does the lawyer he seeks representation accept him at first? Why or why not?

___

___

6. What is Andrew Beckett's profession?

___

___

AFTER VIEWING

1. Have you ever witnessed a person being discriminated for some reason? Talk about it.
2. What kind of discrimination do we mostly witness in our daily lives?
3. Can you give a suggestion of how to avoid discrimination?

AVATAR

Disponível em: <http://www.youtube.com/watch?v=5PSNL1qE6VY>.
Acesso em: 27/09/2011.

BEFORE VIEWING

1. What do you know about the film Avatar?
2. Who directed it?
3. I believe there are different people living on different planets.

☐ I agree ☐ I don't agree

Justify:____

____.

VIEWING

1. What do they offer Jake Sulley?

____

____

2. Why did he become a marine?

____

____

3. What is the name of the place they are going to?

____

4. What is the name of the population they are looking for?

____

5. What specific information did the captain give about the population?

____

____

6. What are the marines looking for? Where is it?

____

____

7. What are Avatars? How are they grown?

____

____

8. What does the captain offer Jake Sulley if he is able to get what the captain needs?

____

____

THE KING'S SPEECH

(O DISCURSO DO REI)

Disponível em: <http://www.youtube.com/watch?v=pzI4D6dyp_o>.
Acesso em: 28/09/2011.

BEFORE VIEWING

1. Have you ever given a speech in public?
2. How do you think people feel when talking in public? Mention four feelings.
3. Do you think it is important to know how to speak in public? Why?
4. How can you learn how to speak in public?

VIEWING

1. What was the first suggestion the therapist gave the King?

____

2. Why couldn't the King do this?

____

3. What did the therapist say he needed from the King in order to cure him?

____

____

4. When asked: "Why are you here then?" what was the King's answer?

____

____

5. In what situation did the King get angry and realized he had a voice?

____

____

AFTER VIEWING

1. How do you deal with speaking in public?

____

____

2. Can you think of a trick to share with everyone to help to speak in public?

____

____

3. Why do you think people stammer?

____

____

DESERT FLOWER

(FLOR DO DESERTO)

Disponível em: <http://www.youtube.com/watch?v=8BhrPUjA6f8&feature=fvsr>. Acesso em: 28/09/2011.

BEFORE VIEWING

Work in pairs.

1. Name 3 things you know about Africa.
2. Do you know what an arranged marriage is? Talk about the pros and cons.
3. What other countries, apart from some regions in Africa, have arranged marriages as part of their culture?
4. Mention some famous people who came from very poor backgrounds and were able to change their lives.

VIEWING

Describe the scene in six sentences.

1. ____________________
2. ____________________
3. ____________________
4. ____________________
5. ____________________
6. ____________________

AFTER VIEWING

1. Talk about a day that changed your life.
2. Do you believe you can make your own destiny?
3. Read this sentence, discuss it with your partner and explain it in your own words: "There is a problem in my country. Whatever happens to the least of us has an effect on all of us. Let's just try to change what that means: to be a woman."

THE SAMURAI
(PART 1/10)

Disponível em: <http://www.youtube.com/watch?v=Qjduob4Fri0&feature=related>. Acesso em: 27/09/2011.

BEFORE VIEWING

1. Think about a completely different culture than your own. Discuss it with a partner.
2. Do you know what a Samurai is?
3. In which country could you find them?

VIEWING

Watch the first 5min30s of this excerpt and answer the questions below.

1. How can you define Samurai?

____

2. How long did they hold the power?

____

3. What weapons did they use and what did they fight for?

____

4. What is Yabusame and how long does it take to become an expert?

____

5. Does a rider sit or stand? Why?

____

6. How was defeat seen amongst the Samurai?

____

7. How big is Japan? How many islands does it have?

____

____

8. What was the first kind of farming that appeared in Japan?

____

AFTER VIEWING

With the information you have so far about Japan and the samurais, write a small paragraph about what you learned.

____

____

____

ATIVIDADES DE

VÍDEO

PARTE 2: FILMES

Atividades de 50 minutos

NAME OF FILM / SITCOM	CONTEXT	VOCABULARY	
1. Madagascar	Animals Zoo	Describing animals, birthday	
2. Finding Nemo [Procurando Nemo]	Sea animals	Colors and descriptions	
3. Shrek	Fantasy world	Seasons, means of transportation, food	
4. Hachiko – A Dog's Tale [Sempre ao seu lado]	Pets and loyalty	Non specific vocabulary	
5. Harry Potter and the Philosopher's Stone [Harry Potter e a Pedra Filosofal]	School	Vocabulary related to school	
6. The Blind Side [Um Sonho Possível]	School and family	Feelings and celebrations	
7. Toy story 3	Donating toys	Toys	
8. Garfield: the movie [Garfield: o filme]	A day in the life of cat	Vocabulary related to routine	
9. The Terminal [O Terminal]	Traveling	Vocabulary and questions related to airports	
10. The Sixth Sense [O Sexto Sentido]	Ghosts and the senses	Vocabulary related to ghosts and secrets	
11. The Devil Wears Prada [O Diabo Veste Prada]	Job interview	Vocabulary related to clothing, adjectives	
12. Juno	Teenage pregnancy	Vocabulary related to adjectives	
13. Avatar	Life on other planets	Vocabulary related to Science fiction Describing feelings, places and scenes	
14. Hitch [Hitch – Conselheiro Amoroso]	Dating and relationships	Physical and personality descriptions, Describing places and facts	
15. The Shawshank Redemption [Um Sonho de Liberdade]	Conviction and prison	Vocabulary related to law and prison	
16. Pretty Woman [Uma Linda Mulher]	Relationships Prejudice and good manners	Vocabulary related to clothes, personality and physical description	
17. How to Lose a Guy in 10 Days [Como Perder um Homem em 10 Dias]	Relationships	Verbs and adjectives related to relationships	
18. Inglorious Basterds [Bastardos Inglórios]	II World War	Non specific vocabulary	
19. Friends – The One with the Embryos – The Roommate Game	Roommate game	Physical descriptions, food	
20. Invictus	Apartheid Leadership	Vocabulary related to the topic	

GRAMMAR/FUNCTIONS AND SKILLS WORKED ON	COMMUNICATIVE/ COMPETENCES	LEVEL
Listening comprehension	Strategic	Basic
Use of modal should Listening comprehension	Strategic	Basic
Listening comprehension	Strategic	Basic
Listening comprehension Imperative	Strategic and grammatical	Basic
Listening comprehension	Strategic	Basic
Listening comprehension Imperatives	Strategic and grammatical	Pre-intermediate
Past tense Use of sequence markers	Strategic, grammatical and discourse	Pre-intermediate
Listening comprehension Present tense Past tense	Strategic, grammatical and discourse	Pre-intermediate
Making questions Use of should	Strategic and grammatical	Pre-intermediate
Listening comprehension and use of past tense	Strategic, grammatical and discourse	Pre-intermediate/intermediate
Listening comprehension, describing people, giving opinions	Strategic, grammatical and discourse	Pre-intermediate
Listening comprehension and giving opinions	Strategic, grammatical and discourse	Pre-intermediate
Listening comprehension Markers (at first, then, after, finally)	Strategic and discourse	Intermediate
Listening comprehension Use of adverbs of frequency Giving instructions Use of imperative	Strategic, grammatical and discourse	Intermediate
Listening comprehension Uses of wish Use of reported speech	Strategic, grammatical and discourse	Intermediate
Listening comprehension Modal verb: should and should not	Strategic and grammatical	Intermediate
Listening comprehension Imperatives using dos and don'ts	Strategic and grammatical	Intermediate
Listening comprehension and the use of If clauses	Strategic and grammatical	Upper intermediate
Listening comprehension Making Trivial Pursuit questions	Strategic and grammatical	Upper intermediate/advanced
Listening comprehension	Strategic and discourse	Advanced

MADAGASCAR

BEFORE VIEWING

In pairs, answer these questions.

1. What's your opinion about animals in the zoo?
2. Is there a zoo in your city?
3. Do you like to go to the zoo?
4. Do you go to the zoo when you travel to different places?
5. What kind of animals are there in zoos?
6. Have you seen any film or cartoon about zoos?
7. Tell your partner what you know about this cartoon.

(00:03:08-00:05:40)

VIEWING

I. Answer these questions.

1. Where are the characters?

___

2. What animals are they?

___

___

3. What are their names?

___

4. Are they happy?

___

5. What other animals can you see?

___

___

II. What are they like? Can you describe the characters by matching them to their characteristics? Each character can have more than one characteristic.

1. Alex	**2.** Gloria	**3.** Melman	**4.** Marty
☐ fat	☐ tall	☐ strong	☐ short legged
☐ energetic	☐ furry	☐ has two wings	☐ long necked
☐ dangerous	☐ enthusiastic	☐ has four legs	☐ spotted
☐ striped	☐ thin	☐ smart	☐ friendly

III. What does the sign near the cage of the monkeys say?

- [ ] Don't feed the animals.
- [ ] Don't step on the grass.
- [ ] Keep your zoo clean.
- [ ] Don't litter.

CHAPTER 3 (00:08:35–00:09:00)

VIEWING

Check True or False. Correct the false statements.

1. Gloria has meat for lunch. ☐ ____________________
2. Marty has grass for lunch. ☐ ____________________
3. Alex has fruit for lunch. ☐ ____________________
4. Melman has medicine for lunch. ☐ ____________________

(00:09:00-00:10:27)

BEFORE VIEWING

How do you celebrate your birthdays? Do you make a wish when you blow the candles?

____

____

____

VIEWING

Answer these questions.

1. Which character is celebrating a birthday today?

   ____

2. How old is he today?

   ____

3. What present did he get from Melman?

   ____

   ____

4. How do they sing "Happy Birthday to you"?

   ____

   ____

   ____

5. What is his wish? He says: "I wish I ______________________________

____."

6. Is it a good idea in Alex's opinion?

____

7. Is it bad luck if you tell your wish?

____

____

CHAPTER 14 (00:57:18-00:58:17)

VIEWING

Where are the characters now?

____

(01:00:50-01:02:40)

VIEWING

Check the correct response.

1. What's Alex doing?
   ( ) He's eating.
   ( ) He's biting Marty's butt.
2. Why is he doing that?
   ( ) He's angry with Marty.
   ( ) He's hungry.
3. What does he see when he looks at them?
   ( ) Animals.
   ( ) Steaks.
4. What happened to Alex?
   ( ) He became wild.
   ( ) He's kidding.

AFTER VIEWING

Talk to your partner and decide where the characters should live: in the wild or in the zoo? Explain why.

☐ They should live ______________________________

because ______________________________

____.

FINDING NEMO

(PROCURANDO NEMO)

BEFORE VIEWING

I. Answer the questions below.

1. Where is Australia? Is it in the southern or northern hemisphere?
2. What's the capital of Australia? Canberra, Sydney or Perth?
3. Which animals represent Australia?

II. Read the paragraph below. Answer the questions in groups of four students.

READING TIP

The Great Barrier Reef is about 1.250 miles long. It is the largest deposit of coral in the world. It is home to approximately 1.500 species of fish, 400 species of coral, 4.000 species of mollusks, 500 species of seaweed, 215 species of birds, 16 species of sea snakes and 6 species of sea turtles. Many animals live there to protect themselves.

1. Where is the Great Barrier Reef located?
2. What kind of animals live in the Australian reefs?
3. Do they need to be protected?
4. Do you remember a cartoon that takes place in Australia?

CHAPTER 3 (00:05:15- 00:08:11)

VIEWING

I. Put the dialogue in the correct order.

☐ Wake up! Wake up!
☐ Not you, dad. Me!
☐ I don't want to go to school. Five more minutes.
☐ Get up! Get up!
☐ First day of school!
☐ It's time for school!
☐ First day of school!

II. Let's talk about Nemo and his dad.

1. How many stripes do they have? 1 2 3
2. Do they have fins? YES NO
3. What color are they? ______________________.
4. What animals does Nemo ask his father about? Circle them.

turtles	fish	birds	mollusks	coral	sharks

III. Bob, Ted and Bill are Nemo's friends from school.
Match and describe them.

1. Bob	octopus
2. Bill	seahorse
3. Ted	fish

1. Bob ______________________________

____

2. Bill ______________________________

____

3. Ted ______________________________

____

CHAPTERS 22/23 (01:10:00-01:15:40)

VIEWING

In pairs, organize the sequence.

- [ ] Darla arrives.
- [ ] Nemo is captured.
- [ ] Marlin and Dori say thank you to the whale.
- [ ] Marlin and Dori arrive to Sydney.

AFTER VIEWING

Talk to your partner.

1. What do you think happens to Nemo, Dori and Marlin?

____

____

2. What should/shouldn't people do to protect this kind of environment?

____

____

____

SHREK

BEFORE VIEWING

I. What's the name of the film?

1. A story about a famous pirate called: ____________________

2. A boy who has powers and can climb buildings: ____________________

3. A man who fights crime in Gotham city: ____________________

4. Mutant superheroes protect the world that hates them: ____________

II. Answer the questions.

1. Do you like cartoons?

____

2. What is your favorite cartoon?

____

3. Do you know Sleeping Beauty?

____

4. What is in the story of Sleeping Beauty?

- ☐ a prince
- ☐ a castle
- ☐ a dragon
- ☐ a baby
- ☐ a frog
- ☐ a swan
- ☐ an ogre
- ☐ a princess

5. Do you know a similar story to Sleeping Beauty but with other characters?

____

CHAPTER 3 (00:00:00-00:00:13)

VIEWING

I. Check the correct answers.

1. What are the names of the ogres and their friend?

☐ Shrek ☐ Rex ☐ Loan ☐ Fiona ☐ Donkey

2. Is Shrek happy when he leaves?

☐ yes ☐ no

3. What is their means of transportation?

☐ car ☐ bus ☐ carriage ☐ boat ☐ donkey

4. What seasons do they go through?

☐ Summer ☐ Winter ☐ Spring ☐ Autumn

5. Does it rain? ☐ yes ☐ no

6. What question does the Donkey always ask?

☐ Do you have a mother? ☐ Are we there yet? ☐ What is your name?

7. Where are they going?

☐ Kingdom of Far Far Away
☐ Kingdom of Cinderella
☐ Kingdom of the donkeys

8. What is there on the way to the castle?

☐ trees ☐ mountains ☐ people ☐ buses ☐ churches

(00:15:00-00:18:33)

VIEWING

1. Who joins them for dinner?

____

2. What is for dinner?

☐ chicken ☐ lobster ☐ banana ☐ hamburger ☐ fish
☐ rice ☐ salad ☐ potatoes ☐ pork ☐ tomato

AFTER VIEWING

I. Choose your favorite character.

1. Shrek	**2.** Fiona	**3.** Donkey

Use these adjectives to justify your choice.

handsome	big	quiet	intelligent	brave	coward
fast	slow	irritating	talkative	patient	elegant

Ex.: I like Shrek. He is strong.

____

II. Answer these questions.

1. Do you think the King and the Queen are like Shrek and Fiona? Why? Why not?

____

2. Do you think the King and Queen are happy with the visit of their daughter?

____

HACHIKO – A DOG'S TALE

(SEMPRE AO SEU LADO)

BEFORE VIEWING

Answer the following questions and report them to a partner.

1. Do you have a pet? What's his/her name?
2. What kind of pet do you have?
3. Do you think a dog can be a man's best friend?
4. What's the best thing about having a pet?

VIEWING

(00:00:35-00:04:00)

I. Watch the first excerpt and answer the questions below.

1. Who's Ronnie's hero?

____

2. Where do you think Hachiko came from?

____

3. What happened to Hachiko?

____

4. Where did he appear?

____

5. Who found him?

____

6. How do you call a baby dog?

____

CHAPTER 4 (00:23:10-00:25:34)

II. Watch this chapter and order the sentences you hear.

- [ ] You ready?
- [ ] Go get it.
- [ ] This is a ball.
- [ ] Come here.
- [ ] Hold on. I need to find a pen.
- [ ] The dog has already been taken.
- [ ] Are you the dog's owner?
- [ ] I'll throw it, you bring it back.
- [ ] I'm really sorry.
- [ ] You can do this.

III. Watch the scene again and answer the questions.

1. Is Wilson happy with Hachiko?

____

2. What's Wilson doing?

____

3. Can Hachiko fetch the ball?

____

4. In your opinion, does Wilson's wife want to keep the dog?

____

____

5. What does she decide to do? Why?

____

____

(00:33:05-00:33:26)

IV. Watch this excerpt and complete the dialogue.

Daughter: Mom.

Mrs. Wilson: Yes, sweety. ______________________________. Hi.

Daughter: Hi. Got the chips.

Mrs. Wilson: Thanks.

Michael: ____________, Mrs. Wilson, __________________.

Mrs. Wilson: Hi, nice to see you. ________________________.

Michael: Ok.

Mrs. Wilson: Thank you, thank you.

Daughter: Looks ______________________________________.

Mrs. Wilson: Oh, good.

Michael: That's a great spread.

Daughter: Why don't you take this to Dad?

Michael: ____.

Mrs. Wilson: He's out back.

Michael: Is the grill ____________________________________?

Mrs. Wilson: It's getting there, yeah. ______________________.

Michael: ____.

Mrs. Wilson: That would be great, honey.

(00:34:25-00:35:25)

V. Watch this excerpt and, in pairs, try to recognize at least 3 expressions you've learnt.

AFTER VIEWING

1. Write down 5 things you think dogs can do.

2. Hachiko goes to the train station to meet Wilson every day but he doesn't fetch the ball. Why is that?

3. Write a paragraph about your pet and what it can do.

HARRY POTTER AND THE PHILOSOPHER'S STONE

(HARRY POTTER E A PEDRA FILOSOFAL)

BEFORE VIEWING

1. What different kinds of schools can you think of?
2. Would you like to attend a different school from the one you are at now? Why? What kind of school would you like to go to?
3. If you could choose, what subjects would you choose to study?

(00:34:00-00:40:00)

VIEWING

Watch the excerpt. Fill out the chart with the information about Harry and about yourself.

	GO TO SCHOOL BY....	BEST FRIEND'S NAMES	YEAR AT SCHOOL	SCHOOL'S NAME	PETS	SUBJECTS STUDIED AT SCHOOL
Harry						
You						

AFTER VIEWING

1. Point out some differences comparing your school to Harry's.

____

2. Are there certain rules in your school? Name some.

____

(00:55:00-00:58:55)

VIEWING

1. What specific instruction did Professor Hooch give her students?

____

2. Did Harry obey? Why or why not?

____

____

AFTER VIEWING

I. Order the following sentences and fill out the missing words.

- [ ] Welcome to your first flying ______________________.
- [ ] With feeling.
- [ ] Good ______________________ class.
- [ ] On my whistle ______________, ______________...
- [ ] Shut up, Harry.
- [ ] When ______________ blow the whistle, ______________ want ______________ to kick off from the ground, hard.
- [ ] Stick your right hand over the broom and say ______________.
- [ ] Neville.
- [ ] Good ______________________, Madame Hooch.
- [ ] Up, up, up.
- [ ] Well, what are ______________ waiting for. Everyone step up to the left side of their broomstick.
- [ ] Come back down this instant Mr. Longbottom.
- [ ] Now, once you've got hold of ______________ broom, ______________ want ______________________ to mount it.
- [ ] Down, down.
- [ ] Keep your broom steady, hover for a moment then lean forward slightly and touch back down.
- [ ] Good afternoon, Amanda. Good ______________________.
- [ ] Come on now, hurry up.
- [ ] Up, up, up.
- [ ] Grip it tight. ______________ don't want to be sliding off the end.
- [ ] Mr. Longbottom, Mr. Longbottom.

II. Now answer (T) for True and (F) for False.

1. [ ] Harry knows how to fly on the broom.
2. [ ] Harry protects Neville.
3. [ ] Harry and Malfoy are friends.
4. [ ] Hermione is good at the first flying class.
5. [ ] Harry obeys Mr. Hooch.
6. [ ] Ron likes Hermione from the first day of school.

THE BLIND SIDE

(UM SONHO POSSÍVEL)

BEFORE VIEWING

1. How do you feel on the first day of school?
2. Do teachers at your school introduce the new students?
3. What do you usually do on your first day of school?

(00:09:11-00:11:40)

I. VIEWING

(NO SOUND)

Observe the excerpt and analyze the image. Talk to a partner. What conclusions can you come to? How does the boy feel? What is his first activity at school?

II. VIEWING

(WITH SOUND)

Watch again and answer the questions. Compare the answers to the first viewing.

1. What place is it? What's its name?

___

2. What's the boy's name?

___

3. What does the teacher ask the students to do?

___

4. Does the boy comfortable?

___

___

5. How do the classmates and teacher feel?

___

___

6. Can the boy do the quiz? What does he do instead?

___

___

___

___

___

(00:14:40-00:15:49)

VIEWING

1. What does Mike try to do?

____

2. How do they react?

____

____

3. What kind of advice does Sean give him?

____

____

4. What's Sean's nickname?

____

____

(00:20:00-00:21:60)

VIEWING

Complete the dialogue with the missing structures.

Leigh Anne: What is he wearing? It's freezing. What's his name again?

SJ: Big Mike.

Leigh Anne: Where is he going?

Sean: Hey Big Mike. Where are you headed?

Mike : Gym.

Sean: ____.

Mom: ______________________ Big Mike. ______________________.

Big Mike. My name is Leigh Anne Tuohy. My kids go to Wingate. You said you were going to the gym. The gym is closed. Why did you say you were going to the gym? Big Mike, why are you doing to the gym?

Mike: Because it's warm.

Leigh Anne: Do you have any place to stay tonight? Don't you dare lie to me.

Sean: I've seen that look many times. She's about to get her way.

Leigh Anne: ______________________, SJ, ______________________.

______________________. ______________________.

Sean: Where are we going?

Leigh Anne: Home.

(00:27:15-00:28:40)

BEFORE VIEWING

Complete the chart. Research on the internet if possible.

	National Holidays	How one celebrates it
In Brazil		
Other countries		

VIEWING

1. What's the main holiday for Americans?

____

2. How do they celebrate it?

____

3. What are the differences and similarities between Thanksgiving in the United States and Christmas in Brazil?

____

AFTER VIEWING

In pairs, talk about what Leigh Anne did. Would you do the same? Would you invite a stranger to stay at your home? Would you adopt a homeless teenager?

____

TOY STORY 3

BEFORE VIEWING

I. In pairs, answer these questions.

1. Which were your favorite toys when you were a child? Name three of them.
2. Do you keep old toys? What do you do with them?

II. Check the toys you have/had.

- [ ] dolls
- [ ] Barbie dolls
- [ ] Ken
- [ ] drums
- [ ] balloons
- [ ] crayons
- [ ] Mr. Potato Head
- [ ] dartboard
- [ ] ball
- [ ] jumping rope
- [ ] Lego
- [ ] wooden toys
- [ ] soldiers
- [ ] plastic animals
- [ ] video games
- [ ] games
- [ ] dice
- [ ] kite
- [ ] puppets
- [ ] board games
- [ ] stuffed animals
- [ ] kaleidoscope
- [ ] robot
- [ ] yo-yos
- [ ] cars
- [ ] dominoes
- [ ] jigsaw puzzles
- [ ] ping pong table and racket
- [ ] Teddy bears
- [ ] magic sets

III. In pairs, tell your partner about tasks I and II and write a small paragraph.

____

____

____

____

____

____

CHAPTERS 4 AND 5 (00:11:42-00:15:25)

VIEWING

I. Andy is going to college next Friday. Watch the excerpt and answer the questions.

1. What does his sister Molly want?

____

____

2. What does Andy's mother want him to do? What are the possibilities?

____

____

____

3. What does Molly decide to donate?

____

____

4. What does Andy decide to do?

____

____

____

5. What happens to the toys?

____

____

6. What happens afterwards? Can they escape?

____

____

II. Order the sequence of sentences.

[1] Mom: Ok, Andy. Let's get to work here. Anything you are not taking to college either goes in the attic or it's trash.

[ ] Mom: Come on. It's garbage day.

[ ] Andy: Mom…

[ ] Andy: Mom, I'm not leaving till Friday.

[ ] Toys: Poor Barbie.

[ ] Andy: Molly, out of my room.

[ ] Mom: Molly , you're not off the hook, either. You have more toys than you know what to do with. Some of them could make other kids really happy.

- [ ] Mom: The children at the daycare. They are always asking for donations.
- [ ] Toys: What's daycare?
- [ ] Molly: Why do you still have these toys?
- [ ] Mom: Fine, You'll have till Friday. Anything that is not packed for college or in the attic is getting thrown out.
- [ ] Molly: But...
- [ ] Mom: Look, it's simple. Skateboard, college. Little league trophy probably attic. Apple core, trash. You can do the rest.
- [ ] Mom: No buts. You choose the toys you want to donate, I'll drop them off at the Sunnyside.
- [ ] Mom: Like what are you going to do with these toys? Should we donate them to Sunnyside?
- [ ] Mom: Maybe sell them online.
- [ ] Molly: What kids?
- [ ] Andy: Mom, none is going to want those old toys. They are junk.
- [ ] Molly: 3 more days and it's mine.
- [ ] Andy: No.
- [ ] Toy: I get the Corvette.
- [ ] Mom: Andy, come on. You have to start making decisions.
- [24] Andy: Whatever you say, mom.
- [ ] Andy: Like what?

AFTER VIEWING

Watch the excerpt again and based on the answers above, tell your partner the sequence of events. Use the words *first, then, after that, finally*. Start with:

Andy is going to college ______________________________

____

____

____

____

____

____

____

____

GARFIELD: THE MOVIE

(GARFIELD: O FILME)

BEFORE VIEWING

1. What kind of film is *Garfield*?
2. Do you like this kind of movie?

(00:00:36-00:04:34)

VIEWING

I. Listen and take notes in the space provided. (no picture)

1. Where does the scene take place?
2. Who are the characters?
3. What is their relationship?
4. What happens in the scene you have just listened to?

II. Answer the questions below. (picture)

1. Where does the scene take place?
2. Who are the characters?
3. What is their relationship?
4. What happens in the scene you have just seen?

III. Put the following sentences in the correct order.

- ☐ Jon hugs Garfield.
- ☐ The alarm goes off.
- ☐ Garfield jumps on Jon.
- ☐ Garfield says "I hate Mondays".
- ☐ Jon takes a shower.
- ☐ Garfield goes out.
- ☐ Garfield uncovers Jon.
- ☐ Garfield jumps on the bed.
- ☐ Garfield is snoring.
- ☐ They have breakfast.

AFTER VIEWING

Now retell the beginning of the story using the past tense. Use exercise II as an input.

____

____

____

____

____

____

(00:00:36-00:04:34)

VIEWING

I. Watch the scene again and answer the questions below.

1. What is the flavor of Garfield's breakfast?

____

2. What happens to Jon's breakfast?

____

3. When does the milk truck come?

____

____

4. Why doesn't Garfield leave the *cul-de-sac*?

____

____

(00:10:27-00:13:05)

VIEWING (NO PICTURE)

I. Listen to the scene (no picture) and put the sentences in the correct order.

- [ ] Come on… let's go for a ride to some place you love. It always leaves you feeling pampered and refreshed.
- [ ] Love me, feed me and never leave me.
- [ ] Did you eat all the four boxes of lasagna?
- [ ] Oh… I know… Chucky Cheese… Thank you. No… Wendy's…
- [ ] It's not my fault. They started it.
- [ ] There is nothing wrong with Garfield. He is just a happy, fat, lazy cat.
- [ ] What am I going to do with you?

II. Talk to a partner and imagine what the scene would be like. Take notes in the space provided. Watch the scene, take notes again and compare your answers.

No picture	Picture

III. Answer the questions below.

1. Why did Jon take Garfield to the Vet?

___

2. What is Jon's relationship with the Vet?

___

3. What does the Vet say about the relationship between Jon and Garfield?

___

4. Since when has Jon had a crush on the Vet?

___

5. What did the Vet give him?

___

THE TERMINAL

(O TERMINAL)

BEFORE VIEWING

1. Do you like travelling?
2. Where do you like to go?
3. Do you like travelling by plane?
4. Where have you traveled to?
5. Which is the biggest airport you have been to?
6. Do you like airports?
7. What can you do there?
8. Fill out the following chart with questions that can be asked in each sector.

Free shop	
Passport Control	
Baggage Reclaim	
Customs	

(00:00:00-00:00:55)

VIEWING

Check the things you see in the first scene.

☐ dogs	☐ people	☐ flags	☐ policemen
☐ benches	☐ plants	☐ doors	☐ baggage belt
☐ tables	☐ booths	☐ bags	☐ names of cities
☐ cameras	☐ children	☐ books	☐ shops

(00:01:00-00:01:25)

VIEWING

1. Write down 3 questions the Passport Control officer asks.

2. Compare your answers with the chart.

(00:01:34-00:03:10)

VIEWING

Put the following scenes in the correct order.

- [ ] Japanese people running.
- [ ] People arriving.
- [ ] Passport Control officer looks at his passport.
- [ ] The Director of Customs looking at the TV monitor.
- [ ] People taking their suitcases off the baggage belt.
- [ ] Mr. Navorski talking to the Passport Control officer.
- [ ] Mr. Navorski shaving.

(00:03:14-00:06:00)

VIEWING

1. What questions does the officer ask him?

2. Does Mr. Navorski understand English?

3. What is the only word Mr. Navorski understands when talking to the Director of Customs?

4. What happened to Mr. Navorski's country?

5. Where is he staying?

(00:08:46-00:10:00)

VIEWING

1. What does the officer give Mr. Navorki? Why?

2. What does he say about America?

3. What is the only thing he can do at this moment in the airport?

AFTER VIEWING

1. Have you heard of a case like this one? Do you think it is possible?

2. Do you think travelling is complicated? Why or why not?

3. Talk to a colleague and list 8 things you should do before travelling.

THE SIXTH SENSE

(O SEXTO SENTIDO)

BEFORE VIEWING

1. Do you believe in ghosts?
2. Do you think there is life after death?
3. How many senses do we have?
4. Which one do you use the most?
5. Which one couldn't you live without? Which one is most important for you?

(01:22:00-01:26:36)

I. VIEWING

SICK GIRL SCENE (NO SOUND)

Read the questions, watch the sequence and take notes in the space provided.

1. Who are the characters?
2. What do you think happened to the girl?
3. How did she die?
4. Who killed her?
5. Why did the boy give the box to the father? How do you think the boy got the box?

(01:22:00-01:26:36)

II. VIEWING

(WITH SOUND)

1. Who are the characters?

___

2. What do you think happened to the girl?

___

3. How did she die?

___

4. Who killed her?

___

5. Why did the boy give the box to the father? How do you think the boy got the box?

___

___

(00:50:14-00:51:30)

BEFORE VIEWING

SECRET SCENE

1. Do you have secrets?

____

2. Do you like to have secrets? Do you share them with anyone?

____

____

____

VIEWING

1. What is the boy's secret?

____

2. How do you think the boy got the box in the scene of the sick girl?

____

____

(00:20:40-00:26:00)

VIEWING

THE GAME SCENE

Put the sentences in the correct order.

- [ ] Wanna sit?
- [ ] How do you draw now?
- [ ] Your dad gave you that watch as a present just before he went away...
- [ ] You're worried that if she said you told him things...
- [ ] Don't feel like talking today?
- [ ] Wanna play a game?
- [ ] You keep pretty quiet at school but you are a good student...
- [ ] You have a secret but you don't want to tell me.
- [ ] You saw that on TV...
- [ ] When your mum and dad were first divorced your mum went to see a doctor like me and he did not help her.

(01:31:06-01:36:00)

VIEWING

LAST SCENE

Complete the sentences with the correct word.

hurt	see	secrets	quiet	lady	important	accident	window
ghosts	talk	freak	face	minute	visit	dance	fight

Mum: I hope nobody got ______________________________.

Mum: You are very __________. You are mad I missed the play, aren't you? I have two jobs, baby. You know how ______________________ they are for us. I'd give anything to have been there.

Cole: I am ready to communicate with you now.

Mum: Communicate?

Cole: Tell you my____________________.

Mum: What is it?

Cole: You know the ___________________ up there?

Mum: Ya.

Cole: Someone got hurt.

Mum: They did?

Cole: A_______________________. She died.

Mum: Oh my god, but you can _______________________ her?

Cole: Yes.

Mum: Where is she?

Cole: Standing next to my _____________________________.

Mum: Cole, you are scaring me.

Cole: They scare me too sometimes.

Mum: They?

Cole: ____

Mum: You see ghosts, Cole?

Cole: They want me to do things for them.

Mum: They ________________ to you, to tell you to do things?

Cole: They're the ones who used to hurt me.

Cole: What are you thinking, mama. You think I am a _________________?

Mum: Look at my ________. I would never think that about you. Ever. Got It?

Cole: Got it.

Mum: Let me just think for a ______________________.

Cole: Grandma says hi! She says she is sorry for taking the bumble pendent. She just likes it a lot.

Mum: What?

Cole: Grandma comes to ________________ me sometimes.

Mum: Cole, that's very wrong. Grandma is gone, you know that.

Cole: I know. She wanted me to tell you...

Mum: Cole, please.

Cole: She wanted me to tell you she saw you _______________, she said when you were little, you and her had a ________________, right before your dance recital. You thought she didn't come to see you dance. She did. She hid in the back so you would not see. She said you were like an angel. She said you came to the place where they buried her, asked her a question, she said the answer is... everyday...

Cole: What did you ask?

Mum: Do I make her proud?

AFTER VIEWING

Talk about a film you have recently seen. Use the past tense.

THE DEVIL WEARS PRADA

(O DIABO VESTE PRADA)

BEFORE VIEWING

1. Have you ever had a job interview?
2. What kind of clothes do you think you should wear for a job interview? Casual or formal?

(00:00:30–00:03:25)

VIEWING

I. Check what you see in this scene.

☐ dresses	☐ skirts	☐ bra	☐ panties
☐ handbags	☐ earrings	☐ lipstick	☐ mascara
☐ scarfs	☐ sneakers	☐ gloves	☐ coats
☐ pullover	☐ stockings	☐ shirt	☐ T-shirt
☐ blouses	☐ eye shadow	☐ fur coat	☐ caps
☐ socks	☐ cosmetics	☐ vest	☐ boots
☐ high heeled shoes		☐ long overcoats	

II. Answer the questions.

1. In which city does this scene take place?

____

2. What's the weather like?

____

3. What kind of transportation does Andy take?

____

4. Andy is going to have a job interview. Is she well dressed?

____

____

5. What should she wear in your opinion? What should she do with her hair?

____

____

____

BEFORE VIEWING

1. How do you feel before a job interview?

____

2. What should you do before a job interview?

____

____

____

CHAPTER 2 (00:03:25–00:04:35)

VIEWING

Check the correct answer.

1. Where is Andy?
   - [ ] At a restaurant.
   - [ ] At a bank.
   - [ ] At the headquarters of a big company.
   - [ ] At a shopping center.

2. How does she feel?
   - [ ] Confident.
   - [ ] Nervous.
   - [ ] Calm.
   - [ ] Happy.
   - [ ] Insecure.

3. What is Runway?
   - [ ] It's a bank.
   - [ ] It's a publishing company.
   - [ ] It's an insurance company.

4. Miranda is
   - [ ] the assistant manager.
   - [ ] the secretary.
   - [ ] editor in chief.
   - [ ] the receptionist.

5. What is Emily like?
   - [ ] Stressed.
   - [ ] Friendly.
   - [ ] Ironic.
   - [ ] Calm.

6. Is Andy interested in fashion? Justify. [ ] yes [ ] no

____

____

BEFORE VIEWING

I. Classify the adjectives in the box below in the correct column.

hard-working	humorous	snobbish	critical	dishonest
polite	imaginative	ambitious	incompetent	calm
experienced	supportive	decisive	generous	sociable
conceited	considerate	well-organized	diplomatic	punctual
stressed	respectful	competent	confident	trustful
helpful	bossy	ironic	rude	intimidating

POSITIVE	NEGATIVE

II. What are the characteristics of an ideal boss?

____

____

____

____

____

CHAPTER 3 (00:04:35-00:06:35)

VIEWING

Watch the sequence and answer the questions.

1. Can you describe the boss? What's she like?
2. How does everybody feel about her?
3. Does Miranda want to see Andy?
4. What does she ask Andy?
5. What does Andy answer?

(00:35:45-00:36:27)

VIEWING

1. Does Andy look different?
2. Compare Andy before and after working for Miranda.

AFTER VIEWING

Do you think a job can change someone's personality?

JUNO

BEFORE VIEWING

Answer the questions below.

1. Have you ever met a teenager who got herself pregnant?
2. If yes, what decision did she take? Did she get married and have the child? Did she give the child up for adoption? Did she decide for an abortion?
3. In your opinion, what should a teenager do if she gets pregnant?
4. Do teenagers have access to sex education?
5. How do parents usually react?
6. Who do you think the teenager should talk to first about her pregnancy?

(00:21:22-00:25:10)

VIEWING

I. Watch this excerpt and check the words that describe best how they feel/react.

Juno feels
- [ ] embarrassed
- [ ] guilty
- [ ] afraid
- [ ] sorry
- [ ] confused
- [ ] determined

Her step mother is
- [ ] calm
- [ ] tense
- [ ] upset
- [ ] worried
- [ ] concerned

Her dad is
- [ ] surprised
- [ ] angry
- [ ] supportive

Lea, her best friend, is
- [ ] cooperative
- [ ] helpful
- [ ] friendly
- [ ] encouraging

II. Watch again and complete the sentence.

Juno decides ______________________ because ______________________.

(00:54:05-00:57:13)

VIEWING

I. Watch the next excerpt **with no sound** and guess what's happening.

____

____

II. Watch again **with sound** and complete the conversation.

Juno: Hi.

Vanessa: Juno.

Juno: Vanessa, what brings you to ______________________?

Vanessa: I was just ______________________ with my girlfriends.

Friend: You're gay?

Juno: Just ignore ______________________.

Vanessa: Oh, no, ______________________.

Vanessa: How ______________ you ______________?

Juno: Great! __________ is stupendous. Coming in on the snooze button.

Vanessa: That's ______________________!

III. Watch it again, check your work and order the dialogue below.

- [ ] What?
- [ ] Are you kidding? Go on.
- [ ] I'm a legend. They call me the cautionary whale.
- [ ] Can you hear me, baby? Sweet angel?
- [ ] I felt it. Oh, God. That was magical.
- [ ] Oh, God.
- [ ] I can't feel anything. It's not moving for me.
- [ ] Could I feel it?
- [ ] Hi, baby. It's me. It's Vanessa. I can't wait to meet you.
- [ ] Kicking away.
- [ ] You should try talking to it because supposedly they can hear you even though it's like 10,000 leagues under the sea.
- [ ] At school everyone is just grabbing my belly all the time. It's crazy!
- [ ] Thank you. Thank you.

AFTER VIEWING

What advice would you give a teenager friend who is starting his/her sexual life?

I think you should ____

____

____

____

____

AVATAR

BEFORE VIEWING

1. Do you like Science?
2. Mention some aspects that you can study in this subject.
3. In what fields do you think Science has advanced the most?
4. Do you believe we can clone people? Physically or mentally?

(00:09:35-00:11:48)

VIEWING

Answer the following questions in the chart below.

What is Jake doing?	
Why?	
What is the concept mentioned?	
What does one of the men comment about good science?	
Who is Grace?	
Does she like Jake at first?	
What language does she ask Norm about?	
Does he speak the language? What about her?	
What happened to Jake's brother?	

AFTER VIEWING

1. What do you think Jake has to do?

____

____

2. Do you believe there are lives on other planets?

____

____

____

(01:04:00-01:04:15)

BEFORE VIEWING

Do you believe in energy between people, plants and animals?

VIEWING

(NO SOUND)

Describe this scene step by step in your own words.

___

___

___

VIEWING

(WITH SOUND)

1. What do the Na'vis believe?

___

___

___

2. Do you believe we are interconnected in some way? People, plants, animals?

___

___

___

(01:18:33-01:21:23)

BEFORE VIEWING

Mention some specific ceremonies we have in our society.

___

___

___

VIEWING

1. Describe Jake's feelings.

___

2. Has he finished his mission according to the colonel?

___

3. Why does he want to continue?

___

___

4. What did the colonel promise him?

5. Was Jake accepted into the Na'vis' society?

6. Describe the ceremony.

7. Describe a Na'vi physically.

8. Transcribe what Jake said about the Na'vis' belief of being born.

AFTER VIEWING

1. Do you believe ceremonies are important?

2. What kind of ceremonies have you participated in?

3. Describe them.

HITCH

(HITCH – CONSELHEIRO AMOROSO)

BEFORE VIEWING

1. What is the culture of dating in your city like?
2. Do girls ask boys out? What is your opinion about that?
3. Where is the best place to meet people?

(00:15:21-00:18:23)

VIEWING

1. Where is the character?

____

2. Name three things you see on the desk.

____

3. Describe him physically.

____

____

4. How would you describe his personality by this scene?

____

____

5. What are their names?

____

6. What is Hitch's occupation?

____

7. What expression does Hitch use to say the other man is crazy?

____

8. Why are they talking?

____

____

9. Do you think it is easy for him to get a girlfriend? Why?

____

____

____

____

____

(00:20:35-00:25:53)

VIEWING

I. Answer the questions.

1. What adverbs of frequency could you hear in this conversation? Write the sentences where they appear below.

____

2. Name the other adverbs of frequency you know and write a sentence with each one of them.

____

II. Answer the questions below about each scene.

IN THE MEETING ROOM

1. Professional relationship between Albert and Allegra.

____

2. Describe the meeting room.

____

3. Subject talked about.

____

4. Albert's reaction in the meeting.

____

5. Outcome.

____

6. Expression used by Albert to say he was leaving his job.

____

____

IN ALBERT'S OFFICE

7. Subject talked about.

____

8. Body language used in this conversation. Give examples of other body language you constantly use and see others using.

____

9. Describe Albert's feelings before and after Allegra's entrance.

____

____

10. Tell your partner what Allegra said using reported speech.

____

(00:49:33-00:50:50)

BEFORE VIEWING

DANCING SCENE

1. Do you like dancing?
2. Do men like dancing or do women like dancing more?
3. Do you think you dance well?

VIEWING

(NO SOUND)

1. Describe the scene.

____

____

____

2. Give clear instructions to your partner explaining how to dance like Albert.

____

____

3. Is Hitch happy? Why?

____

____

AFTER VIEWING

1. Are there any principles in relationships? Are there rights and wrongs and dos and don'ts?

____

____

2. Make a list of dos and don'ts of a first date and discuss it with your partner. Make sure you use adverbs of frequency and clear instructions (imperative).

____

____

____

____

____

____

____

____

____

THE SHAWSHANK REDEMPTION

(UM SONHO DE LIBERDADE)

BEFORE VIEWING

1. Together with a partner, describe a prison in 5 words.
2. Describe what kind of people are in a prison.
3. List 5 reasons why a person can be convicted.
4. How do you think people smuggle things into prison?
5. Should you trust your first impressions about people?

(00:06:22-00:07:20)

VIEWING (NO SOUND)

Watch the scene and create a dialogue between the men.

____

____

____

____

____

____

____

VIEWING (WITH SOUND)

Put the following sentences in the correct order.

- [ ] You feel you have been rehabilitated?
- [ ] Sit.
- [ ] Yes, sir.
- [ ] Oh, yes sir. Absolutely, sir. I mean I have learnt my lesson.
- [ ] I can honestly say I am a changed man, I am no longer a danger to society. That's God's honest truth.
- [ ] We see by your file you have served 20 years of a life sentence.

(00:07:20-00:13:45)

VIEWING

1. What does Red (Morgan Freeman) smuggle into the prison?

____

____

2. What did Andy ask Red to smuggle into the prison?

____

____

3. What year did Andy arrive in the prison?

____

4. What was he convicted for?

____

____

5. What was his previous job?

____

____

6. Did Red like Andy at first sight? What was his first impression?

____

____

7. What is the warden's name?

____

____

8. What are the instituition's beliefs?

____

9. Are good friendships possible to be made in a prison?

____

____

(02:12:53-02:15:45)

VIEWING

I. Complete the sentences with the idioms or words.

1. If you are reading this it means that you have ____________________.
2. I could use ____________________ to get my project ____________________ .
3. I will ____________________.
4. ____________________ is a good thing, and good things never ____________________.

   I am hoping that this ____________________ finds you well.

II. Retell the scene using indirect speech.

____

____

____

AFTER VIEWING

I. Rewrite the sentences using *wish*.

Example:

Andy regrets he married.

Andy wishes he had not gotten married.

1. Red misses Andy.

____

____

2. The prisoners are fighting and Red would like them to stop.

____

____

3. Andy wants to buy a hotel but he does not have enough money yet.

____

____

4. Red regrets having fought with an intern yesterday.

____

____

5. Red has no cigarettes and he regrets that.

____

____

II. Answer the question.

Do you agree with the prison system in your country? In groups, discuss other ways you believe are possible to rehabilitate people who have been convicted of a crime. Use *I wish* whenever possible.

____

____

____

____

____

____

____

____

PRETTY WOMAN
(UMA LINDA MULHER)

BEFORE VIEWING

Based on the title, what do you think this film will be about?

____

____

(01:39:00-01:45:00)

VIEWING

1. What is Phil and Edward's relationship?

____

2. What is Mr. Morse and Edward's relationship?

____

3. What does Edward do to make Mr. Morse more comfortable?

____

4. What are Edward's intentions towards Mr. Morse's company? What are his words?

____

____

____

5. How does Mr. Morse finish the conversation?

____

6. Complete the chart.

How Phil said Edward spoiled the deal	
Two words Phil uses to describe Vivian	
What does Vivian suggest guys learn in high school?	

7. What do you think Edward and Vivian's relationship is?

____

____

____

(00:31:11–00:36:19)

BEFORE VIEWING

Do you think good manners are important? Why?

VIEWING

1. Describe Edward and Vivian.

	PERSONALITY CHARACTERISTICS	PHYSICAL CHARACTERISTICS
Edward		
Vivian		

2. How does Edward hint to Vivian about been educated?

3. Describe Edward's job.

4. Describe Vivian's job.

5. What does Vivian compare Edward's job to?

6. What proposition does Edward make to Vivian?

7. For how much do they close the deal?

(00:40:18-00:41:20)

BEFORE VIEWING

SHOPPING SCENE

1. Are dress codes important?
2. In pairs, discuss what you would wear for:

   a. an evening wedding:____________________

   b. an informal lunch:____________________

   c. to go shopping:____________________

   d. a barbecue:____________________

3. Have you ever been looked down upon for what you were wearing?

VIEWING

1. How do the people treat Vivian in the shop?
2. Do you agree with the shop attendants?
3. Why should one dress appropriately?
4. Answer True or False.

   a. ☐ Edward and Vivian are related.
   b. ☐ Edward wants to do business with Mr. Morse.
   c. ☐ Vivian wants to please Edward.
   d. ☐ Edward lives in a hotel.
   e. ☐ Phil likes Vivian.

AFTER VIEWING

Write down 5 things we should do and 5 things we should not do when at a fancy restaurant.

HOW TO LOSE A GUY IN 10 DAYS

(COMO PERDER UM HOMEM EM 10 DIAS)

BEFORE VIEWING

Answer the questions in pairs.

1. Have you ever had a boy/girlfriend? Have you ever fallen in love?
2. Complete the chart with Dos and Don'ts a woman/man should do or should not do to keep a relationship healthy. Use the ideas below. You can add extra ideas.

   Be clingy, cool, act needy, be fun, whiny, smart, use baby talk, be always beautiful/ handsome, talk about babies, talk about marriage, be obsessed about old boyfriends/girlfriends, appear on the boys'/girls night, prepare "yummy" snacks, ask him/her not to smoke, disturb the boys'/girls' games, talk to his/her mother behind his/her back, take him/her to a concert, act insane, get along fine with his/her parents, go to places both like, be charming, look good all the time, be polite.

DOS	DON'TS

CHAPTER 13

VIEWING

I. Watch the first part of the scene (Girls talking – 00:59:54-01:00:50)

1. Take notes about everything Andy's friends suggested.

   ____

   ____

2. Has Andy done everything?

   ____

3. What do Andy's friends tell her to do?

   ____

II. Watch the second part of the scene (The boy's night – 01:00:50-01:06:30).

1. What are the boys doing?

____

____

2. How did she get Ben's key to the apartment?

____

3. What does she do to disturb them?

____

____

____

____

____

4. Compare what she did to the preview chart. Are there any coincidences?

____

____

____

____

____

5. Complete with True or False. Correct the false sentences.

a. ☐ They are playing a board game. ______________________

b. ☐ They are eating pizza. ______________________

c. ☐ The fern is doing well. ______________________

d. ☐ Andie is insane. ______________________

e. ☐ Ben thinks Andie is acting different. ______________________

f. ☐ Ben's dog is sleeping. ______________________

AFTER VIEWING

1. Talk to a partner and imagine how the movie ends. Do they break apart? Do they stay together?

2. Write a paragraph about it.

____

____

____

____

____

____

INGLORIOUS BASTERDS

(BASTARDOS INGLÓRIOS)

BEFORE VIEWING

In groups of 3, answer the following questions.

1. What do you know about World War II?
2. When did the war begin and end?
3. How did the war end? Who won the war?
4. What were the belligerents called?
5. What happened in France?
6. Who were Hitler, Goebbels, Göring and Bormann?

CHAPTER 23 (02:03:35-02:10:24)

VIEWING

I. Hans Landa, a Nazi German colonel is talking to Aldo Raine, an American jewish first lieutenant and Utivich, who were caught by the Germans. Watch the scene and do the following activities.

1. What are the nicknames given to the three men?

   Aldo: ______________________________

   Hans Landa: ______________________________

   Utivich: ______________________________

2. Does Colonel Landa agree with his nickname? What does he say about it?

   ____

   ____

   ____

3. Did Utivich know he was called Little Man? Was he surprised?

   ____

   ____

II. Match the words to their meanings.

1.	mercy	☐	unable to move, fixed
2.	stuck	☐	to stop fighting and accept defeat
3.	catchy	☐	damaged
4.	kaput	☐	something easy to remember
5.	surrender	☐	kindness that makes you forgive someone

III. Match the expressions to their meanings.

1. "looks like the shoe is on the other foot"
2. "..... you get what you pay for"
3. "it's still a go"
4. "to make a deal"
5. "I've done my share of bootlegging"
6. "long story short"

- [ ] someone is experiencing what they used to make others experience, normally negative things
- [ ] acted illegally
- [ ] make an arrangement, an agreement
- [ ] receive what you deserve
- [ ] to summarize
- [ ] proceeding, operating

IV. Watch the excerpt again and complete the sentences.

1. If I were sitting where you are sitting,____________________ you ____________________ (show) me mercy?
2. If you get all 4, you ____________________(end) the war tonight.
3. If you want to end the war tonight, we ____________________ (have) to make a deal.
4. If I were sitting in your chair, I ____________________ probably________ ____________________ (say) the same thing.

V. What does colonel Landa want to do? What's his idea?

____

____

____

____

AFTER VIEWING

Talk to a partner and decide whether lieutenant Aldo will make the deal with colonel Landa. Present your ideas to the class.

THE ONE WITH THE EMBRYOS – THE ROOMMATE GAME

BEFORE VIEWING

1. Have you ever had a roommate?
2. Describe your perfect roommate.
3. What are the problems one might have when we are sharing an apartment?
4. In what situation and what period of life do people usually have roommates?

(00:00:00-00:02:50)

VIEWING

Watch the first excerpt and work in pairs.

1. Why is Monica mad?

____

____

____

2. What does Joey suggest Monica's wearing?

____

3. Describe what a friend of yours is wearing.

____

4. How many items are there in Rachel's bag?

____

5. What are the items?

☐ apples	☐ cookies	☐ fruit	☐ milk
☐ chips	☐ yogurt	☐ soda	☐ oranges

6. What is the last item in Rachel's bag?

____

7. What do they bet?

____

8. Why did Rachel buy it?

____

____

____

9. Make a list of 10 items you can buy in a grocery store.

10. How much do they bet the second time?

- [ ] 2 bucks
- [ ] 200 bucks
- [ ] 100 bucks
- [ ] 10 bucks

11. What kind of game do they suggest?

12. Do they bet? How much?

13. How many questions do they have to answer?

14. Name three categories.

15. Give 3 different suggestions as how to choose who will start a game. How do they choose?

16. Check 5 expressions you hear.

- [ ] Do you wanna bet?
- [ ] How do you know?
- [ ] So not true!
- [ ] You're good.
- [ ] So not impressed.
- [ ] I am so scared.
- [ ] Fork it over.
- [ ] Deal!
- [ ] Completely out of hand.

AFTER VIEWING

Let's play Trivial Pursuit!

INVICTUS

BEFORE VIEWING

1. In pairs, talk about the meaning of the word apartheid.
2. Do you know who Nelson Mandela is?

CHAPTER 1 (00:00:58-00:02:11)

VIEWING

Nelson Mandela was released from prison after 27 years.

1. Describe what you see.

____

____

2. What does the expression "go to the dogs" mean?

____

____

(00:02:11-00:04:20)

VIEWING

1. When was Mr. Mandela released from prison?

____

2. What happened according to the news on TV?

____

____

____

3. What does Mr. Mandela tell the people to do?

____

____

4. What did the black population of South Africa do for the first time in 1994?

____

____

____

5. Complete the sentence by President Mandela:

"Never, never and ____________________ shall it be that this will again experience the ____________________ of one by another and suffer the ____________________ of being the skunk of ____________________."

(00:45:39-00:51:16)

BEFORE VIEWING

In groups of 4, talk about the position of a leader. Is it difficult? How do leaders inspire their team/ people/ employees to do their best? How can a leader inspire his/her team to be better?

VIEWING

François Pienaar, captain of the South African rugby team is invited to see President Mandela.

1. What have the English given the South Africans according to President Mandela?

____

2. What do they talk about?

____

3. Where did President Mandela find inspiration when he was arrested at Robben Island and he was in despair?

____

____

4. How did François inspire his team before the games?

____

____

5. What song did President Mandela hear in Barcelona in 1992 during the Olympic Games that inspired him to go back home and do his best?

____

____

(01:12:00-01:15:00)

VIEWING

Watch part of a rugby game. In the film it was the first World Cup game against Australia. Talk to a partner. After that, answer the questions.

1. Is it similar to any other sports you know?

____

____

2. Who won the game?

____

____

(01:16:00-01:21:00)

VIEWING

After winning the first game against Australia, François decides to take the team to visit the Robben Island and see where Mr. Mandela was kept for 27 years (1964-1990). Listen to the poem Mr. Mandela used to read while he was there. Order the sequence of the poem.

- [ ] I thank whatever gods may be
- [ ] I have not winced nor cried aloud
- [ ] Beyond this place of wrath and tears
- [ ] It matters not how strait the gate
- [ ] Looms but the Horror of the shade
- [ ] In the fell clutch of circumstance
- [ ] Finds and shall find, me unafraid
- [ ] Out of the night that covers me
- [ ] My head is bloody, but unbowed.
- [ ] I am the master of my fate.
- [ ] Black as the Pit from pole to pole
- [ ] I am the captain of my soul.
- [ ] For my unconquerable soul
- [ ] Under the bludgeoning of fate
- [ ] And yet the menace of the years
- [ ] How charged with punishment the scroll

AFTER VIEWING

Watch the whole film and write at least 5 sentences answering the following questions: Why did President Mandela decide to support the South African rugby team? What was his main goal?

____

____

____

____

____

____

____

____

____

SINOPSES, INFORMAÇÕES TÉCNICAS, *TEACHING TIPS* E *ANSWER KEY*

PARTE 1: *TRAILERS*

Atividades de 20 minutos

THE TOURIST
(O TURISTA)

Disponível em: <http://www.youtube.com/watch?v=GrqpKEOF8uw&feature=related>. Acesso em: 20/09/2011.

INFORMAÇÕES TÉCNICAS
Lançamento: 2010, EUA, França
Direção: Florian Henckel von Donnersmarck
Elenco: Angelina Jolie e Johnny Depp
Gênero: Thriller
Duração: 2min22s

SINOPSE

Um turista americano (Johnny Depp) conhece uma mulher misteriosa (Angelina Jolie) que o leva para um mundo perigoso de intriga e espionagem. Quando Frank encontra Elise no trem, pensa que seja por acaso. Aos poucos ele percebe que foi envolvido em um plano maior que se desenvolve nas ruas históricas de Paris e nos canais de Veneza.

TEACHING TIPS

Esta é uma atividade que pode ser utilizada como *warm-up* se você estiver abordando assuntos como viagens ou meios de transporte. Antes de mostrar o *trailer*, organize a classe em pares e peça que respondam às perguntas do *Before viewing* para ativar o conhecimento prévio dos alunos. Em seguida, peça que leiam as perguntas (*Viewing*) e assistam ao *trailer*. Os alunos podem fazer a correção comparando suas respostas com outro par. Mostre o *trailer* novamente para que completem o diálogo e peça que, a partir do diálogo, deduzam o significado das expressões.

Faça o *After viewing* se houver tempo. Coloque os alunos em pares, reveja os advérbios de frequência e peça que organizem as palavras no quadro. Em seguida peça que interajam a respeito da frequência com que usam os meios de transporte.

ANSWERS

BEFORE VIEWING

Open answers.

VIEWING

I.

1. Angelina Jolie and Johnny Depp.
2. Elise and Frank.
3. Thriller.
4. On a train.
5. Venice.
6. Train, plane, subway, speedboat and gondola.
7. She introduces him as her husband.

II.

Frank: I need help / the door
Receptionist: What kind

III.

1. to smash the door
2. to enter illegally by criminals

IV. (open answer)
Ex.: The man broke down the door because he forgot his key.
The criminals broke into my house.

AFTER VIEWING

1.

In the air: zeppelin, airplane, helicopter, hot air, balloon; **In the water:** hovercraft, speed boat, gondola, ship; **On the road:** train, bus, bike, motorbike, scooter, truck, car, subway.

2.

Open answers.
Ex.: I always catch a bus to go to school.
I rarely fly a plane.

OCEANS
(OCEANOS)

Disponível em: <http://www.youtube.com/watch?v=ARFH4aXYFFM>. Acesso em: 22/09/2011.

INFORMAÇÕES TÉCNICAS
Lançamento: 2010, França, Suíça, Espanha
Duração: 2min32s

SINOPSE

Oceanos é um documentário épico produzido pela Disney Nature. Aproximadamente três quartos da superfície terrestre são cobertos por água, e o filme explora as histórias e mistérios que neles se escondem. Os diretores mergulharam fundo nas águas que sustentam a vida humana, explorando o esplendor e as duras realidades das criaturas marinhas, filmadas com a mais avançada tecnologia de captação de imagens subaquáticas.

TEACHING TIPS

Essa atividade pode ser utilizada como *warm-up* para introduzir animais marinhos e abordar o Dia da Terra. É importante utilizar as perguntas do *Before viewing* para ativar o conhecimento prévio dos alunos. Leia e explique as perguntas para os alunos. Lembre-se de que se eles forem de nível básico as respostas poderão ser dadas na língua materna. São sugestões e podem variar de acordo com o nível do grupo. Aceite respostas objetivas também. O vídeo pode ser mostrado duas ou três vezes. A atividade deve tomar no máximo 15 minutos.

Site extra para consulta com ilustrações de *sea animals*: <http://www.languageguide.org/english/vocabulary/sea-animals/>. Acessado em 27/09/2011.

ANSWERS

BEFORE VIEWING

1. April 22nd.
2. Earth Day celebrates our planet Earth: the plants, the animals that live here with us. This holiday reminds us to appreciate nature and learn ways to protect it. It started being celebrated in 1970 in the USA.
3. Open answer.
4. Open answer.
5. 70% of the planet is covered by water: 1.260.000.000.000.000.000.000 liters.
6. Some examples: whale, fish, shark, jelly fish, sea turtle.

VIEWING

1. sharks; whales; fish; turtles; jelly fish; seagulls; dolphins; ray; squid; seal; walrus; octopus; pelican; school of fish; iguana; penguins.
2. Less than 5%.

AFTER VIEWING

1. Recycle; save water; save electricity; use recycled products; use shopping bags instead of plastic bags; don't pollute; don't throw garbage in the sea, on the streets.
2. Some ideas: I recycle paper, plastic, glass and metal; I recycle garbage; I take my old clothes to charity; I avoid buying plastic; I plant trees; I save water; I save electricity.

FRIENDS – SEASON 4 – EPISODE 4

THE ONE WITH THE BALLROOM – AT THE GYM

Disponível em: <http://www.youtube.com/watch?v=C_ESeEZD_OY>. Acesso em 27/09/2011.

INFORMAÇÕES TÉCNICAS
Lançamento: 1994, EUA
Criadores: Marta Kauffman, David Crane e Kevin S. Bright
Produtores: Kevin S. Bright, Marta Kauffman, David Crane, Shana Goldberg-Meehan e Scott Silveri
Elenco: Jennifer Aniston (Rachel Green), Courteney Cox Arquette (Monica Geller), Lisa Kudrow (Phoebe Buffay), Matt Le Blanc (Joey Tribbiani), David Schwimmer (Ross Geller), Matthew Perry (Chandler Bing)
Gênero: Comédia
Duração: 2min23s

SINOPSE

Friends, um clássico seriado de humor que contou com 10 temporadas (1994-2004), girava em torno de um grupo de seis amigos inseparáveis que viviam na área de Manhattan, na cidade de New York. Possui muitos fãs pelo mundo inteiro, pois todos que assistem conseguem se identificar com algum personagem e não se cansam de rir, seja com a mimada e bela Rachel; a sistêmica e cheia de manias Mônica; a divertida, desafinada e louca Phoebe; o mais lerdo, Joey; o divertido e reprimido, Chandler; e, por fim, o inteligente e cheio de decepções amorosas, Ross.

Neste episódio, Chandler quer parar de frequentar a academia, mas não consegue devido às atraentes funcionárias do local. Ross, que inicialmente deveria ajudar Chandler a parar de frequentar, no final se torna um membro da academia.

TEACHING TIPS

Essa atividade pode ser utilizada para introduzir vocabulário relacionado a esportes para o nível básico. Um *brainstorming* de esportes pode ser feito no *Before viewing*.

Para o nível intermediário, pode ser introduzido o estudo de maneiras de se posicionar com relação ao tema. Por exemplo, na terceira questão os alunos podem usar: *In my opinion...; I think...!; I agree...; I don't agree...; I totally disagree...*

No *Viewing* leia as questões com os alunos antes de assistir ao vídeo.

ANSWERS

BEFORE VIEWING

Open answers.

VIEWING

1. F; 2. F; 3. F; 4. T; 5. T.

AFTER VIEWING

1. Open answer.
2. Possible answers: language courses, a job, a relationship etc.
3. Possible answers: In my opinion, when it becomes boring; ...when it becomes too difficult.

RIO

Disponível em: <http://www.youtube.com/watch?v=P1GRO31ve5Q&NR=1>. Acesso em: 28/09/2011.

INFORMAÇÕES TÉCNICAS
Direção: Carlos Saldanha
Vozes: Anne Hathaway, Jesse Eisenberg; George Lopez, Tracy Morgan, Jemaine Clement, Leslie Mann, Jamie Foxx
Lançamento: 2011, EUA
Gênero: Animação
Duração: 2min47s

SINOPSE

O filme *Rio* conta a história de Blu, uma arara-azul rara que pensa que é a última de sua espécie. Quando Blu descobre que há uma "outra" arara-azul, ele deixa o conforto de sua gaiola em uma pequena cidade de Minnesota e vai para o Rio de Janeiro para conhecer Jewel. Inesperadamente juntos, embarcam em uma aventura em que aprendem sobre amizade, amor, coragem e sobre estar aberto às muitas maravilhas da vida. *Rio* reúne personagens vibrantes, uma história comovente, mergulhos coloridos, uma música latina contemporânea e cheia de energia.

TEACHING TIPS

O filme aborda a questão dos animais que correm risco de extinção. Discuta esse tópico com os alunos e situe o filme nesse contexto. Organize a classe em pares e peça que respondam às primeiras perguntas antes de assistir ao *trailer*. Em seguida, peça que alguns alunos reportem o que conversaram, principalmente quanto à terceira questão. Se a atividade for usada com grupos de nível básico, o *Before viewing* pode ser feito na língua materna.

Leia as perguntas da primeira tarefa do *Viewing* antes de mostrar o vídeo. É importante que os alunos as entendam bem para assistir ao *trailer* com objetividade. Pode ser que eles precisem ver mais de uma vez para completarem as demais tarefas. Peça que façam a atividade colocando os eventos em ordem cronológica e em seguida relacionem as personagens. Se necessário mostre ainda mais uma vez antes de fazer a última atividade.

ANSWERS

BEFORE VIEWING

1. Some monkeys, gorillas, whales, bears, jaguars, bats.
2. Some lose their habitats, some are killed, some are victims of pollution.
3. Donate money to help protect the endangered species, become a member of some societies, work as a volunteer in a zoo or park.
(For more information: <http://www.wcs.org/saving-wildlife.aspx>. Acesso em 28/09/2011.)

VIEWING

I.

1. He can't fly.
2. He lives in Minnesota, USA.
3. He goes to Rio de Janeiro, Brazil.
4. You can see the Christ Statue, the city of Rio de Janeiro, carnival parades, many colorful birds and hear the Brazilian music.
5. He meets another blue macaw called Jewel.

II.

1. Blu brushes his teeth.
2. Blu goes to Rio.
3. Blu meets Jewel.
4. Blu and Jewel escape from the cage.
5. Blu and Jewel fall on a hang glider.
6. Blu and Jewel fall on the beach.

III.

1. the male macaw.
2. the female macaw.
3. the American girl.
4. the Brazilian guy.
5. the toucan.
6. the dog.

IV.

1. Linda; **2.** Tulio; **3.** Tulio; **4.** Blu; **5.** Blu; **6.** Jewel; **7.** Jewel; **8.** Blu; **9.** Rafael; **10.** Luiz.

THE SOCIAL NETWORK
(A REDE SOCIAL)

Disponível em: <http://www.youtube.com/watch?v=P1GR031ve5Q&NR=1>. Acesso em: 28/09/2011.

INFORMAÇÕES TÉCNICAS
Lançamento: 2010, EUA
Direção: David Fincher
Elenco: Jesse Eisenberg, Andrew Garfield, Justin Timberlake, Rooney Mara.
Gênero: Drama
Duração: 2min31s

SINOPSE

Em uma noite de outono em 2003, Mark Zuckerberg (Jesse Eisenberg), analista de sistemas graduado em Harvard, senta-se em seu computador e começa a trabalhar em uma nova ideia. Apenas seis anos e 500 milhões de amigos mais tarde, Zuckerberg torna-se o mais jovem bilionário da história com o sucesso da rede social Facebook. O sucesso, no entanto, leva-o a complicações em sua vida social e profissional.

TEACHING TIPS

Essa é uma atividade rápida de *warm-up* que pode ser feita no início de uma aula cujo tema seja internet, computador ou redes sociais. Contextualize o assunto perguntando aos alunos o que eles mais fazem quando estão conectados. Pergunte-lhes quantas vezes por dia eles se conectam. Organize a classe em pares, leia as perguntas do *Before viewing* com os alunos e peça que respondam às perguntas. Mostre o *trailer* e peça que coloquem as sentenças em ordem. No *After viewing* peça que respondam individualmente e em seguida organize os alunos em pares para que compartilhem suas respostas.

ANSWERS

BEFORE VIEWING

1. Suggestions: I like it; I don't like it; it's useful; it's boring; it's a waste of time; it's addictive etc.
2. To socialize with friends; to share blogs, photographs, sites and other information; to meet new friends; to send messages, to chat etc.
3. Pros: you are connected to the world; you can meet new friends; you socialize etc.
Cons: You are exposed; you can get addicted.
4. Facebook, Orkut, Linkedin, Twitter etc.
5. Open answer.
6. Mark Zuckerberg sat down one night in his room at Harvard and began idealizing Facebook.

VIEWING

(6) Thousand... Twenty-two thousand
(4) People want to go on the internet and check out their friends so why not build a website that offers that friends pictures, profiles... I am talking about taking the entire social experience of college and putting it online.
(8) Millions?
(1) I need to do something substantial in order to get the attention of the clubs.
(7) This idea is potentially worth millions of dollars.
(2) Why?
(5) You got twenty-two hundred hits within two hours?
(9) You stole our website.
(3) Because they are exclusive and fun and lead to a better life.

AFTER VIEWING

Open answers.

PHILADELPHIA
(FILADÉLFIA)

Disponível em: <http://www.youtube.com/watch?v=cl4B9AU45P4>. Acesso em: 28/09/2011.

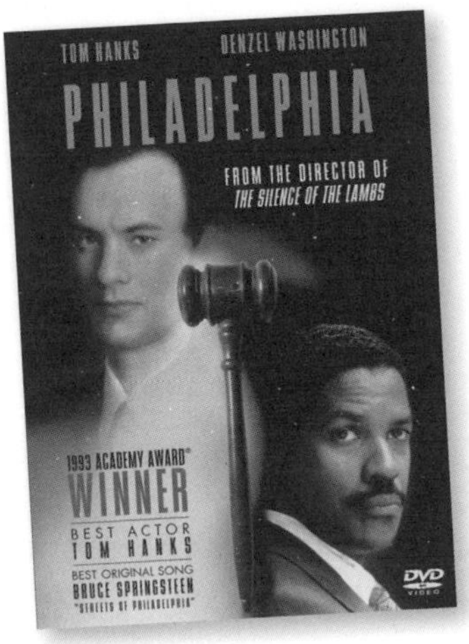

INFORMAÇÕES TÉCNICAS
Lançamento: 1993, EUA
Direção: Jonathan Demme
Elenco: Tom Hanks (Andrew Beckett), Denzel Washington (Joe Miller), Roberta Maxwell (Judge Tate)
Gênero: Drama
Duração: 3min03s

SINOPSE

Promissor advogado (Tom Hanks) que trabalha para tradicional escritório da Filadélfia é despedido quando descobrem ser ele portador do vírus da AIDS. Ele contrata os serviços de um advogado negro (Denzel Washington), que é forçado a encarar seus próprios medos e preconceitos. Os dois competentes advogados juntam forças para processar a prestigiada firma de advocacia pela discriminação da doença. E, alimentados por sua improvável mas crescente amizade, superam com coragem o preconceito e a corrupção de seus poderosos adversários.

TEACHING TIPS

Esse pode ser um assunto delicado. É importante que você conheça bem seus alunos antes de fazer essa atividade. Esse vídeo pode ser usado para contextualizar a questão da discriminação. Organize a classe em pares e peça que discutam as perguntas do *Before viewing*. Abra a discussão para a classe antes que assistam ao *trailer*. Leia as perguntas do *Viewing* com os alunos e peça que respondam em pares, trocando ideias. Coloque os alunos em pequenos grupos para responderem às perguntas do *After viewing*.

ANSWERS

BEFORE VIEWING

1. Discrimination is a prejudicial treatment of a person. It can be related to religion, race, height, nationality, disease, age, gender etc.
2. Ignoring them, hurting them physically or emotionally, making fun of them etc.
3. Open answer.

VIEWING

1. A big corporation.
2. Andrew Beckett. He had just got a promotion.
3. AIDS.
4. He discovered 8 months before.
5. No, he does not. He is scared of even touching him.
6. He is a lawyer.

AFTER VIEWING

1. Open answer.
2. Possible answers: racial, appearances, diseases, nationality, religious.
3. Possible answers: talk about the matter, expose individuals to different cultures and opinions, talk about individuality, promote diversity etc.

AVATAR

Disponível em: <http://www.youtube.com/watch?v=5PSNL1qE6VY>. Acesso em: 27/09/2011.

INFORMAÇÕES TÉCNICAS
Lançamento: 2009, EUA, Inglaterra
Direção: James Cameron
Elenco: Sam Worthington, Sigourney Weaver, Michelle Rodriguez, Zoe Saldana, Giovanni Ribisi, Joel Moore
Gênero: Ação
Duração: 3min32s

SINOPSE

Avatar é um filme americano de ficção científica. A história se passa no ano 2154 e é baseada em um conflito em Pandora, uma das luas de Polifemo, um dos três planetas gasosos fictícios que orbitam o sistema Alpha Centauri. Em Pandora, os colonizadores humanos e os Na'vi, nativos humanoides, entram em guerra pelos recursos do planeta e pela continuação da existência da espécie nativa. O título do filme refere-se aos corpos Na'vi-humanos híbridos, criados por um grupo de cientistas por meio de engenharia genética para interagir com os nativos de Pandora.

TEACHING TIPS

Esse *trailer* pode ser utilizado como *warm-up* para uma aula sobre ficção científica ou sobre vida em outros planetas. Converse com os alunos sobre esses assuntos. Discuta com eles suas crenças sobre vida em outros planetas. Na questão 3 do *Before viewing* os alunos podem conversar em pares. Peça que justifiquem suas respostas. Leia as perguntas do *Viewing* com os alunos antes de assistir ao vídeo. Sugerimos que apresente somente o áudio sem a imagem para que os alunos exercitem a compreensão auditiva. Peça que respondam às perguntas. Em seguida apresente novamente, agora com a imagem, para que tenham uma segunda oportunidade de responder às perguntas. Assista uma terceira vez para verificar as respostas.

ANSWERS

BEFORE VIEWING

Open answers.

VIEWING

1. A fresh start. A new world.
2. For the hardship. He told himself he could pass any test a man could pass.
3. Pandora.
4. Na'vi.
5. They are very hard to kill.
6. A little grey rock. Underneath the Na'vi's village.
7. Remote controlled bodies. They are grown from human DNA mixed with the DNA of the natives.
8. His legs back.

THE KING'S SPEECH
(O DISCURSO DO REI)

Disponível em: <http://www.youtube.com/watch?v=pzI4D6dyp_o>. Acesso em: 28/09/2011.

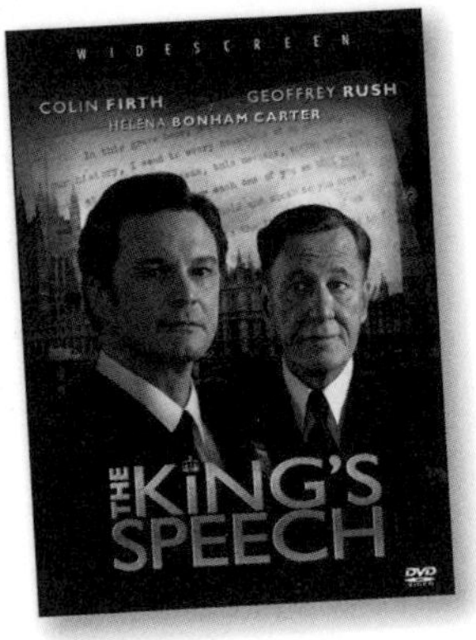

INFORMAÇÕES TÉCNICAS
Lançamento: 2010, Inglaterra
Direção: Tom Hooper
Elenco: Colin Firth, Helena Bonham Carter, Geoffrey Rush, Michael Gambon
Gênero: Drama
Duração: 2min28s

SINOPSE

Desde os 4 anos, George (Colin Firth) é gago. Esse é um sério problema para um integrante da realeza britânica, que frequentemente precisa fazer discursos. George procurou diversos médicos, mas nenhum deles trouxe resultados eficazes. Quando sua esposa, Elizabeth (Helena Bonham Carter), leva-o até Lionel Logue (Geoffrey Rush), um terapeuta de fala de método pouco convencional, George está desesperançoso. Lionel se coloca de igual para igual com George e atua também como seu psicólogo. Seus exercícios e métodos fazem com que George adquira autoconfiança para cumprir o maior de seus desafios: assumir a Coroa após a abdicação de seu irmão David (Guy Pearce).

TEACHING TIPS

Essa é uma atividade rápida de *warm-up* que pode ser utilizada para contextualizar o tema: falar em público. Converse com os alunos usando as perguntas do *Before viewing*. Peça-lhes que citem alguma pessoa famosa que fale bem em público e também uma pessoa que precise melhorar suas técnicas de oratória. Em seguida, peça que assistam ao vídeo e respondam às perguntas do *Viewing*. Os alunos poderão compartilhar as respostas em pares. Oriente-os a prestarem atenção na pronúncia das personagens. Pergunte se é muito diferente da que estão acostumados a ouvir. No *After viewing*, peça que respondam às perguntas individualmente e em seguida abra para o grupo.

ANSWERS

BEFORE VIEWING

1. Open answer.
2. Some examples: nervous, frightened, excited, anxious, calm.
3. Open answer.
4. Take specific courses, practice etc.

VIEWING

1. To change jobs.
2. Because he would be King.
3. Total trust.
4. "Because I bloody well stammer".
5. When the therapist sat on King Edward's chair.

AFTER VIEWING

1. Open answer.
2. Choose a person in the audience and focus your attention mostly on this person, speak slowly, breathe, take small breaks between sentences, choose some expressions you feel comfortable with etc.
3. Because they get nervous; because they do not know the subject well; because they have psychological issues etc.

DESERT FLOWER
(FLOR DO DESERTO)

Disponível em: <http://www.youtube.com/watch?v=TCpXLQTQepo&feature=player_embedded#at=41>. Acesso em: 29/09/2011.

INFORMAÇÕES TÉCNICAS
Lançamento: 2011, EUA, França, Áustria
Direção: Sherry Horman
Elenco: Liya Kebede, Sally Hawkins, Craig Parkinson, Meera Syal, Anthony Mackie, Juliet Stevenson, Timothy Spall, Soraya Omar-Scego, Teresa Churcher, Eckart Friz, Anna Hilgedieck, Matt Kaufman
Gênero: Drama
Duração: 2min01s

SINOPSE

Waris Dirie, nascida numa família nômade no deserto da Somália, sofreu mutilação genital como muitas garotas de sua tribo. Para fugir de um casamento não desejado, aos 13 anos atravessa a pé o deserto africano até chegar à capital, Mogadíscio, e daí a Londres. Apesar de ter uma vida inicialmente acidentada, Waris, já em Londres, se torna uma modelo de projeção internacional. Ela também se tornou embaixadora especial das Nações Unidas na luta pela erradicação da mutilação genital feminina. O filme é baseado no *best-seller* autobiográfico de Waris Dirie.

TEACHING TIPS

Observar que as atividades de *Before viewing* são importantes para levantar o conhecimento prévio dos alunos. Converse sobre a Somália e a Etiópia e peça que imaginem como deve ser a vida em um ambiente tão árido e pobre. O *trailer* pode ser assistido mais de uma vez para que os alunos façam a atividade do *Viewing*. Faça uma pausa após cada cena e peça que os alunos construam uma sentença relacionada a ela. O *After viewing* pode ser feito em grupos de três alunos para que haja mais interação. Peça que os alunos reportem o que foi discutido.

ANSWERS

BEFORE VIEWING

1. There are many poor regions in Africa. It has different cultures. They speak many different languages and dialects. There are many deserts.
2. Pros: You will have the same background. The risk of incompatibility is diminished: you belong to the same culture, you have the same religious upbringing, you speak the same language and you belong to the same economical class. It has a lower divorce rate.
Cons: There might be a big age difference; love takes a second priority; arranged marriages are used as a mean to suppress women marrying them off at a young age, before they become independent. The parents take the decision. It encourages the cast system.
3. Iran, Iraq, Japan, India, Afghanistan and others.
4. Possible answers: Naomi Campbell, Lula, Oprah, Jennifer Lopez, Elvis Presley, Ronaldo.

VIEWING

1. She lived in the deserts of Africa.
2. Her marriage was arranged.
3. She ran away and crossed the desert.
4. She was discovered in a fast food restaurant by a photographer.
5. She wasn't able to walk wearing high heels.
6. She became a top model.

AFTER VIEWING

1. Open answer.
2. Open answer.
3. Possible answer: Women in Africa are discriminated. She can, as an individual, help change this reality. What affects the minority has a big impact on the society as a whole. Africa has to understand what it is to be a woman.

THE SAMURAI
(PART 1/10)

Disponível em: <http://www.youtube.com/watch?v=TCpXLQTQepo&feature=player_embedded#at=41>. Acesso em: 29/09/2011.

SINOPSE

Este documentário de 100 minutos do History Channel explora o legado extraordinário da arte marcial, da cerimônia, da autodisciplina e da persistência dos samurais, que permanecem até hoje. Este primeiro trecho do filme mostra um pouco da história dos Samurais.

TEACHING TIPS

No *Before viewing*, converse com seus alunos sobre a cultura japonesa e o que eles sabem a respeito. Pergunte se alguém já foi ao Japão ou se tem algum conhecido que segue as tradições japonesas. Pergunte sobre outras culturas que sejam muito diferentes da nossa.

Leia as perguntas do *Viewing* antes de assistir ao vídeo e levante hipóteses de respostas com os alunos. Você pode dividir as perguntas do *Viewing* em 2 partes: inicialmente, as perguntas de 1 a 3 (de 00:00-01:00), em seguida as perguntas de 4 a 8 (de 01:00-05:30). Pare o vídeo após cada etapa e peça que os alunos respondam às perguntas. Você pode optar por assistir ao vídeo todo ou parar aos 5min30s.

No *After viewing* oriente os alunos a conversarem em pares sobre o que eles mais gostaram do vídeo. Em seguida, como *homework*, peça que escrevam um parágrafo sobre o que aprenderam.

INFORMAÇÕES TÉCNICAS
Lançamento: 2003, The History Channel, EUA
Duração: 9min53s

ANSWERS

BEFORE VIEWING

1. Open answer.
2. A Samurai is a knight from medieval Japan.
3. Japan.

VIEWING

1. Knights of medieval Japan.
2. 700 years.
3. Sword and bow. They fought for land, status, honor and power.
4. It is a ceremonial and sacred form of mounted archery. It keeps back a tradition of warriors that dates back 1300 years. It takes 3 years to become an expert but most of them have been practicing for 10 to 15 years.
5. He stands. A rider keeps all the weight on his feet and not on the saddle. This way his legs absorb the up and down movement of the horse and it keeps his aim stable.
6. They would commit suicide to preserve ones honor in case of defeat.
7. Roughly the size of the state of California. It has 4 main islands surrounded by hundreds of smaller ones.
8. Rice farming.

AFTER VIEWING

Open answer.

SINOPSES, INFORMAÇÕES TÉCNICAS, *TEACHING TIPS* E *ANSWER KEY*

PARTE 2: FILMES

Atividades de 50 minutos

MADAGASCAR

INFORMAÇÕES TÉCNICAS
Direção: Eric Darnell, Tom McGrath
Vozes: Ben Stiller (Alex, o leão), Chris Rock (Marty, a zebra), David Schwimmer (Melman, a girafa), Jada Pinkett Smith (Gloria, a hipopótamo).
Lançamento: 2005, EUA
Gênero: Animação

SINOPSE

O leão Alex (Ben Stiller) é a grande atração do zoológico do Central Park, em Nova York. Ele e seus melhores amigos, a zebra Marty (Chris Rock), a girafa Melman (David Schwimmer) e a hipopótamo Gloria (Jada Pinkett Smith), sempre passaram a vida em cativeiro e desconhecem o que é morar na selva. Curioso em saber o que há por trás dos muros do zoológico, Marty decide fugir para explorar o mundo. Ao perceberem a fuga do amigo, Alex, Gloria e Melman decidem partir à sua procura. O trio encontra Marty na estação Grand Central do metrô, mas, antes que consigam voltar para casa, são atingidos por dardos tranquilizantes e capturados. Eles são embarcados em um navio rumo à África, onde serão colocados em liberdade por um grupo de humanos que quer tirar os animais da vida estressante em cativeiro. Um grupo de pinguins também está no navio, e todos vão parar na ilha de Madagascar, onde precisam encontrar meios de sobrevivência em uma selva verdadeira.

TEACHING TIPS

Antes de fazer as atividades, é importante contextualizá-las. As do *Before viewing* devem ser bem exploradas. Traga um mapa para localizar a África do Sul e Madagascar. Use a língua-alvo se possível durante toda a atividade e peça aos alunos que o façam também. Leia as perguntas antes de propor cada atividade, para que os alunos assistam ao vídeo com objetivos claros. Depois de terminarem cada tarefa, peça que alguns alunos reportem o que fizeram. Observe que nessa atividade desenvolveremos a competência estratégica dos alunos, ao pedir que respondam às perguntas com base no visual e no auditivo. No *After viewing* peça que os alunos em pares decidam onde as personagens devem viver, justificando sua escolha e, em seguida, completem a sentença.

ANSWERS

BEFORE VIEWING

Open answers.

(00:03:08-00:05:40)

VIEWING

I.

1. At the Central Park Zoo, in New York.
2. A lion, a zebra, a hippo and a giraffe.
3. Alex, Marty, Gloria and Melman.
4. Yes, they look happy.
5. Penguins and monkeys.

II.

1. Alex: strong, energetic, furry, enthusiastic, has four legs, smart, friendly.
2. Gloria: fat, strong, has four legs, short legged, friendly.
3. Melman: tall, has four legs, spots, long necked, thin, friendly.
4. Marty: strong, energetic, enthusiastic, has four legs, striped, friendly.
Obs.: None of the animals have 2 wings or is dangerous or spotted.

III.

Keep your zoo clean.

CHAPTER 3 (00:08:35-00:09:00)

VIEWING

1. F; fruit; **2.** T ; **3.** F; meat; **4.** T.

(00:09:00-00:10:27)

BEFORE VIEWING

Open answer.

VIEWING

1. It's Marty's birthday.
2. He's 10.
3. A thermometer.
4. Happy birthday to you, you live in a zoo, you look like a monkey and you smell like one too.
5. "I wish I could go to the wild."
6. No, it's not.
7. Marty thinks so.

CHAPTER 14 (00:57:18-00:58:17) VIEWING

They are in Madagascar.

(01:00:50-01:02:40) VIEWING

1. He's biting Marty's butt.
2. He's hungry.
3. Steaks.
4. He became wild.

AFTER VIEWING

They should live IN THE WILD because THEY BELONG TO THE WILD.
or
They should live IN THE ZOO because THEY FEEL HAPPY THERE.

FINDING NEMO
(PROCURANDO NEMO)

INFORMAÇÕES TÉCNICAS
Lançamento: 2003, Austrália, EUA
Direção: Andrew Stanton
Vozes: Albert Brooks (Father), Willem Dafoe (Gil), Ellen DeGeneres (Dory), Alexander Gould (Nemo), Barry Humphries (Shark), Geoffrey Rush (Nigel)
Gênero: Animação

SINOPSE

Nemo (Alexander Gould) é um filhote de peixe-palhaço e o único sobrevivente de sua família. Por esse motivo, seu pai (Albert Brooks) é superprotetor. Durante uma excursão da escola, Nemo é capturado por um humano e passa a viver em um aquário. Decidido a encontrá-lo, seu pai se junta a Dori (Ellen DeGeneres) e sai em sua busca.

TEACHING TIPS

Um dos tópicos explorados nesta atividade é a proteção do meio ambiente. Se possível, traga um mapa da Austrália para poder mostrar onde se encontram os recifes de corais. É interessante explorar o tópico com os alunos usando as perguntas de um a três do *Before viewing*. Em seguida, leia com eles as perguntas relativas ao texto para que possam retirar as informações com objetividade. Não cite o nome do vídeo, pois a última questão se refere ao filme.

Para a seção *Viewing*, mostre as sequências mais de uma vez e pare em alguns pontos para que os alunos possam fazer a descrição dos animais usando cores e tamanhos e verificar se responderam corretamente.

No *After viewing* faça com os alunos um levantamento de ações para proteger o meio ambiente. Enfatize o uso do modal should. Observe que, nessa atividade, desenvolveremos a competência estratégica dos alunos ao pedir que ordenem a sequência de eventos e respondam às perguntas com base no visual e no auditivo.

ANSWERS

BEFORE VIEWING

I.

1. It's in the southern hemisphere.
2. It's Canberra.
3. The koala and the kangaroo.

II.

1. In Australia.
2. Fish, coral, mollusks, birds, snakes and turtles.
3. Yes, they do.
4. Yes, *Finding Nemo*.

CHAPTER 3 (00:05:15-00:08:11) → VIEWING

I.

(1) Wake up! Wake up!
(4) Not you, dad. Me!
(3) I don't want to go to school. Five more minutes.
(5) Get up! Get up!
(7) First day of school!
(6) It's time for school!
(2) First day of school!

II.

1. 3
2. yes
3. orange, white and black.
4. turtles; sharks

III.

1. Bob; seahorse
2. Bill; fish
3. Ted; octopus
1. Bob: Yellow, has a long nose.
2. Bill: Blue and yellow, has a long nose.
3. Ted: purple, round, has big eyes, has small ears.

CHAPTERS 22/23 (01:10:00-01:15:40) → VIEWING

1. Marlin and Dori arrive to Sydney.
2. Marlin and Dori say thank you to the whale.
3. Nemo is captured.
4. Darla arrives.

→ AFTER VIEWING

1. Open answer.
2. People shouldn't throw garbage in the sea; people should recycle; people should save energy and water; people shouldn't pollute the environment.

SHREK

INFORMAÇÕES TÉCNICAS
Lançamento: 2001, EUA
Direção: Andrew Adamson
Vozes: Mike Myers (Shrek), Eddie Murphy (Burro), Cameron Diaz (Princesa Fiona), John Lithgow (Lorde Farquaad), Vincent Cassel (Monsieur Hood)
Gênero: Animação

SINOPSE

Em um pântano distante vive Shrek (Mike Myers), um ogro solitário que vê sua vida ser invadida por uma série de personagens de contos de fada, como três ratos cegos, um grande e malvado lobo e ainda três porquinhos que não têm onde morar. Todos eles foram expulsos de seus lares pelo maligno Lorde Farquaad (John Lithgow). Determinado a recuperar a tranquilidade de antes, Shrek resolve encontrar Farquaad e com ele faz um acordo: todas as personagens poderão retornar aos seus lares se ele e seu amigo Burro (Eddie Murphy) resgatarem uma bela princesa (Cameron Diaz), que é prisioneira de um dragão. Porém, quando Shrek e o Burro enfim conseguem resgatar a princesa, eles descobrem que seus problemas estão apenas começando.

TEACHING TIPS

Faça uma competição entre os alunos com as questões do *Before viewing*. Organize a classe em grupos. O grupo que acertar mais ganha. É importante ler sempre as questões antes de assistir ao vídeo para que os alunos o façam com mais objetividade. Observe se há dúvidas de vocabulário. Nas atividades contemplamos vocabulário relativo à alimentação, meios de transporte e estações do ano. Se você estiver desenvolvendo esse vocabulário durante suas aulas, reforce nesse momento.

No *After viewing*, escreva os nomes das três personagens em três cantos da sala. Peça que os alunos escolham o seu preferido e justifiquem usando adjetivos. Observe que nas atividades desenvolveremos a competência estratégica dos alunos ao pedir que ordenem e respondam às perguntas com base no visual e no auditivo.

ANSWERS

BEFORE VIEWING

I.

1. Pirates of the Caribbean.
2. Spiderman.
3. Batman.
4. Transformers.

II.

1. Open answer.
2. Open answer.

3. Open answer.
4. a prince; a castle; a dragon; a baby; a princess.
5. Yes, *Shrek*.

CHAPTER 3 (00:00:00-00:00:13) → VIEWING

I.

1. Shrek; Fiona; Donkey
2. no
3. carriage
4. Summer; Winter; Spring; Autumn
5. yes
6. Are we there yet?
7. Kingdom of Far Far Away
8. trees, mountains, people

(00:15:00-00:18:33) → VIEWING

1. Donkey
2. lobster; fish; pork

→ AFTER VIEWING

I.

1. Open answer.
2. Open answer.
3. Open answer.

II.

1. No, they are very different from each other. Shrek and Fiona are easygoing. The King and Queen are more reserved.
2. No, they are not. They do not accept Fiona as an ogre.

HACHIKO – A DOG'S TALE
(SEMPRE AO SEU LADO)

INFORMAÇÕES TÉCNICAS
Lançamento: 2009, EUA, Inglaterra
Direção: Lasse Hallström
Elenco: Joan Allen, Richard Gere, Sarah Roemer, Jason Alexander, Cary-Hiroyuki Tagawa, Erick Avari, Davenia McFadden
Gênero: Drama

SINOPSE

Quando Hachiko, um filhote de cachorro da raça Akita, é encontrado perdido em uma estação de trem por Parker (Richard Gere), ambos se identificam rapidamente. O filhote acaba conquistando todos na casa de Parker, mas é com ele que acaba criando um profundo laço de lealdade. Baseado em uma história real, *Sempre ao Seu Lado* é um emocionante filme sobre lealdade.

TEACHING TIPS

Esse vídeo pode ser utilizado para levantar o conhecimento prévio a respeito de animais de estimação e sua relação com seus donos. São quatro pequenos trechos que podem ser vistos mais de uma vez, dependendo da necessidade dos alunos. Sugerimos que, a cada trecho, os alunos mudem seus pares.

O *Before viewing* pode ser feito em pares e depois aberto para a classe toda.

Observe que há uma atividade que cita o imperativo. Se você estiver desenvolvendo esse ponto gramatical em sala, reforce e mostre seu uso e amplie utilizando outros exemplos como: *Open the door*, *Close the window*, *Come to the board*, *Sit down*, *Stand up*, *Turn on the lights* etc.

No *After viewing* peça que os alunos pensem a respeito do que os cães são capazes de fazer (pegar bolas, sentar, rolar, ficar em duas patas etc.). Nesse momento os alunos poderão usar a língua materna se necessário. Em seguida peça que reflitam a respeito do que Hachiko consegue fazer e o que não consegue fazer e expliquem o porquê. Na atividade seguinte os alunos escrevem sobre as habilidade de seus animais de estimação . Se eles não tiverem animais peça que escrevam sobre o animal de algum amigo. Essa atividade pode ser feita em casa.

ANSWERS

BEFORE VIEWING

Open answers.

VIEWING

(00:00:35-00:04:00)

I.

1. Hachiko is his hero. He was his grandfather's dog.
2. Japan.

3. He got lost.
4. At the train station.
5. Wilson, Ronnie's grandfather.
6. Puppy.

CHAPTER 4 (00:23:10-00:25:34)

II.

1. This is a ball.
2. I'll throw it, you bring it back.
3. You ready?
4. Go get it.
5. Come here.
6. You can do this.
7. Are you the dog's owner?
8. Hold on. I need to find a pen.
9. The dog has already been taken.
10. I'm really sorry.

III.

1. Yes, he is.
2. He's teaching the dog to fetch the ball.
3. No, he can't.
4. No, she doesn't.
5. She decides to keep the dog because her husband's really happy.

(00:33:05-00:33:26)

IV.

Mrs. Wilson: ... I'm here.
Michael: Hi ... Good to see you.
Mrs. Wilson: ... Call me Kate, thank you.
Daughter: ... delicious.
Michael: Sure.
Michael: ... ready?
Mrs. Wilson: ... Nice to see you.
Michael: Me too.

(00:34:25-00:35:25)

V.

Get the ball; Go get it; Look at...

AFTER VIEWING

1. Roll over, stand up, fetch the ball, fetch the newspaper, sit.
2. Hachiko is an Akita. Akitas don't fetch balls. Collies fetch balls but not Akitas. They are not into people-pleasing.
3. Open answer.

HARRY POTTER AND THE PHILOSOPHER'S STONE
(HARRY POTTER E A PEDRA FILOSOFAL)

INFORMAÇÕES TÉCNICAS
Lançamento: 2001, EUA, Inglaterra
Direção: Chris Columbus
Elenco: Daniel Radcliffe, Rupert Grint, Emma Watson, Richard Harris, Maggie Smith, Robbie Coltrane, Alan Rickman, Ian Hart
Gênero: Aventura

SINOPSE

Harry Potter (Daniel Radcliff) é um garoto órfão de 10 anos que vive infeliz com seus tios, os Dursley. Repentinamente, ele recebe uma carta contendo um convite para ingressar em Hogwarts, uma famosa escola especializada em formar jovens bruxos. Inicialmente, Harry é impedido de ler a carta por seu tio Valter (Richard Griffiths), mas logo ele recebe a visita de Hagrid (Robbie Coltrane), o guarda-caça de Hogwarts, que o leva até a escola. A partir de então, Harry passa a conhecer um mundo mágico que jamais imaginara, vivendo diversas aventuras com seus mais novos amigos, Rony Weasley (Rupert Grint) e Hermione Granger (Emma Watson).

TEACHING TIPS

No *Before viewing*, faça um levantamento com os alunos sobre estilos diferentes de escolas. Por exemplo, pergunte sobre a escola de seus pais. Essas perguntas podem ser respondidas na língua materna, pois o objetivo é contextualizar. Questione se eles sabem algo a respeito do bruxinho Harry Potter e se eles acham que uma escola como a dele poderia existir. Faça as atividades sempre levando em conta o perfil de seus alunos, a fim de introduzir o assunto de acordo com a realidade deles. Os alunos devem assistir ao trecho mais de uma vez para ordenar e completar as sentenças.

Na atividade do *After viewing*, peça aos alunos que comparem suas escolas com a de Harry Potter, mencionando suas matérias escolares e conversando sobre diferentes meios de transporte para ir à escola. Observe que desenvolveremos a competência estratégica dos alunos, ao pedir que ordenem e respondam às perguntas com base no visual e no auditivo.

ANSWERS

BEFORE VIEWING

1. Schools that emphasize music, sports or a specific area; religious schools; boarding schools; boys' schools; girls' schools; military schools; private schools; public schools etc.
2. Open answer.
3. Open answer.

(00:34:00-00:40:00) ➡ VIEWING

	Go to school by....	Best friend's names	Year at school	School's name	Pet	Subjects studied at school
Harry	Train	Ron and Hermione	First year	Hogwarts	Frog	Magic
You	Open answer	Open answer	Open answer	Open answer	Open answer	Open answer

➡ AFTER VIEWING

1. Open answer.
2. Wear uniform, don't speak on the cell phone, respect the other etc.

(00:55:00-00:58:55) ➡ VIEWING

1. Not to take their feet off the floor. Not to fly.
2. No, he did not. Malfoy irritated him

➡ AFTER VIEWING

I.

(4) Welcome to your first flying lesson.
(9) With feeling.
(1) Good afternoon, class.
(16) On my whistle three, two...
(11) Shut up, Harry.
(14) When I blow the whistle, I want you to kick off from the ground, hard.
(7) Stick your right hand over the broom and say up.
(19) Neville.
(2) Good afternoon, Madame Hooch.
(10) Up, up, up.
(5) Well, what are you waiting for. Everyone step up to the left side of their broomstick.
(20) Come back down this instant Mr. Longbottom.
(12) Now, once you've got hold of your broom, I want you to mount it.
(18) Down, down.
(15) Keep your broom steady, hover for a moment then lean forward slightly and touch back down.
(3) Good afternoon, Amanda. Good afternoon.
(6) Come on now, hurry up.
(8) Up, up, up.
(13) Grip it tight. You don't want to be sliding off the end.
(17) Mr. Longbottom, Mr. Longbottom.

II.

1. T; **2.** T; **3.** F; **4.** F; **5.** F; **6.** F.

THE BLIND SIDE
(UM SONHO POSSÍVEL)

INFORMAÇÕES TÉCNICAS
Lançamento: 2009, EUA
Direção: John Lee Hancock
Elenco: Sandra Bullock, Tim McGraw, Quinton Aaron, Kathy Bates
Gênero: Drama

SINOPSE

O adolescente Michael Oher (Quinton Aaron) sobrevive sozinho como um sem-teto, quando é encontrado na rua por Leigh Anne Tuohy (Sandra Bullock). Tomando conhecimento de que o garoto é colega de turma de sua filha, Leigh Anne insiste que Michael – que veste apenas bermuda e camiseta em pleno inverno – deixe-a resgatá-lo do frio. Sem hesitar por um momento sequer, ela o convida a passar a noite em sua casa. O que começa com um gesto de bondade evolui para algo maior, pois Michael passa a fazer parte da família Tuohy, apesar de terem origens bem diferentes. Vivendo no novo ambiente, o adolescente tem de encarar outros desafios. À medida que a família ajuda Michael a desenvolver todo o seu potencial tanto no campo de futebol americano quanto fora dele, sua presença conduz todos por uma jornada de autodescoberta. Esse filme foi baseado em fatos reais.

TEACHING TIPS

Observar que as atividades de *Before viewing* são importantes para levantar o conhecimento prévio dos alunos e reforçar o vocabulário relacionado a *feelings*: *happy*, *sad*, *curious*, *shy*, *confident* etc. Peça aos alunos que citem outros sentimentos que possam ter no primeiro dia de aula. O primeiro *Viewing* é feito sem som. Esse tipo de atividade estimula a criatividade e imaginação. Na atividade de completar o diálogo, perguntar que tempo verbal está sendo usado (imperativo). Chamar a atenção dos alunos para a personalidade de Leigh Anne. Ela é *bossy* (mandona), mas não perde a doçura. Pergunte aos alunos que palavra pode ser usada para deixar o imperativo mais polido. A palavra é *please*, usada no final da sentença. Se você estiver apresentando o item gramatical "imperativo", aproveite para reforçá-lo nesse momento.

No segundo *Before viewing* faça um levantamento com os alunos dos principais feriados nacionais do Brasil e pergunte quais eles conhecem de outros países. Se possível peça a eles que façam uma pesquisa na internet. Converse sobre as diferentes maneiras de celebrar essas datas.

Incentive os alunos a assistir ao filme inteiro em casa. É uma história verídica de adoção e superação de um menino de rua. O *After viewing* pode ser discutido em classe explorando o tema adoção e usado como atividade escrita em casa.

ANSWERS

BEFORE VIEWING

1. Open answer. Possible answers: I feel happy, sad, shy, confident, curious.
2. Open answer.
3. Possible answers: Write about vacation, start studying new topics, review topics studied the year before, take tests, meet new classmates.

(00:09:11-00:11:40)

I. VIEWING (NO SOUND)

Possible answers: It is the character's first day at school. He is curious and shy. He is given a test.

II. VIEWING (WITH SOUND)

1. It's a school. It's called Wingate Christian School.
2. His name is Mike Oher.
3. She asks them to make him feel welcome.
4. No, he doesn't. It seems everything is new for him.
5. They seem curious about the boy.
6. No, he can't. He just draws a boat.

(00:14:40-00:15:49) VIEWING

1. He tries to approach some kids.
2. They run away. They look afraid of him.
3. He tells him to smile at the girls so as they know he's a friend.
4. SJ for Sean Junior.

(00:20:00-00:21:60) VIEWING

Sean: Go ahead.
Mom: Turn around; Stop the car.
Leigh Anne: Come on; make room. Get inside. Come on.

(00:27:15-00:28:40) BEFORE VIEWING

	National Holidays	How one celebrates it
In Brazil	Christmas New Year's Eve	Family get together. Exchange of presents. Fireworks.
Other countries	Israel: Rosh Hashanah (New Year) Britain: Easter Monday, Boxing day. (day after Christmas). American: 4th of July.	Family get together. Parades and fireworks.

VIEWING

1. Thanksgiving.
2. It's a family celebration. Usually a family dinner or a barbecue.
3. Open answer. Christmas and Thanksgiving are both family celebrations. Usually the families get together for a meal.
Thanksgiving originally had a religious significance. Nowadays Americans and Canadians offer thanks on this day and usually eat turkey, corn and pumpkin pie. There are also parades on this day. It's celebrated on the 4th Thursday of November so it's always on different dates.
Christmas is a religious date always on the 25th of December. Brazilians also gather the families for a supper and we eat turkey, pork, rice, pasta and lots of desserts.

AFTER VIEWING

Open answer.

TOY STORY 3

INFORMAÇÕES TÉCNICAS
Lançamento: 2010, EUA
Direção: Lee Unkrich
Vozes: Tom Hanks (Woody), Michael Keaton (Ken), Joan Cusack (Jessie), Tim Allen (Buzz), Blake Clark (Slinky).
Gênero: Animação

SINOPSE

Andy irá para a faculdade e terá que decidir o que fazer com seus brinquedos: se vai jogá-los fora, guardá-los no sótão ou doá-los a uma instituição. Ele resolve guardar seus brinquedos e colocá-los em um saco (exceto Woody, que irá para a faculdade). Porém sua mãe confunde o saco que deveria ir para o sótão com um saco de lixo, e os brinquedos acabam na sarjeta. Quando os brinquedos conseguem escapar do saco de lixo, Woody explica que Andy os guardaria no sótão, mas ninguém acredita e eles acabam indo para a creche Sunnyside. Quando chegam a Sunnyside, todos os recepcionam muito bem, e os brinquedos veem uma chance de melhorar de vida. Porém Woody, que nunca concordou em abandonar Andy, sai da creche e tenta voltar para casa. Os brinquedos descobrem que Sunnyside não é tão legal quanto pensavam.

TEACHING TIPS

Leia com os alunos as perguntas do *Before viewing*. Converse a respeito do tópico com a classe toda. Peça, em seguida, que assinalem os brinquedos. Organize os alunos em pares e peça que conversem sobre os brinquedos comentados nas perguntas 1 e 2. Explique-lhes que a atividade 3 será feita utilizando o tempo passado. Faça um levantamento dos verbos que poderão ser usados. Exemplifique a tarefa na lousa e peça aos alunos que a façam individualmente.

As atividades do *Viewing* podem ser feitas individualmente e depois corrigidas em grupo. Peça que os alunos leiam as perguntas antes de assistir ao vídeo. Mostre a sequência mais de uma vez. No *After viewing*, os alunos utilizarão os marcadores de sequência *first, then, after that* e *finally*. Faça um exemplo com eles na lousa e peça que completem a atividade. Reforce que esse parágrafo será feito usando o tempo verbal presente.

ANSWERS

BEFORE VIEWING

I. Open answers.
II. Open answers.
III.
Suggestion: When I was a child I used to have a..., a... and a... My favorite toy was a... I didn't keep my toys. I donated them/ put them in the trash/ I gave them to...

CHAPTERS 4 AND 5 (00:11:42-00:15:25)

VIEWING

I.

1. She wants his stereo, computer and videogames.
2. She wants him to decide what to do with his things. He can put them in the trash, donate them to daycare or sell them online.
3. She decides to donate her Barbie, a xylophone and a ball.
4. He decides to take Woody to college and put the other toys in the attic.
5. By mistake, they are put in the trash.
6. Yes, they escape and decide to go to daycare.

II.

(1) Mom: Ok, Andy. Let's get to work here. Anything you are not taking to college either goes in the attic or it's trash.
(3) Mom: Come on. It's garbage day.
(4) Andy: Mom...
(2) Andy: Mom, I'm not leaving till Friday.
(15) Toys: Poor Barbie.
(7) Andy: Molly, out of my room.
(9) Mom: Molly, you're not off the hook, either. You have more toys than you know what to do with. Some of them could make other kids really happy.
(11) Mom: The children at the daycare. They are always asking for donations.
(12) Toys: What's daycare?
(6) Molly: Why do you still have these toys?
(23) Mom: Fine, You'll have till Friday. Anything that is not packed for college or in the attic is getting thrown out.
(13) Molly: But....
(5) Mom: Look, it's simple. Skateboard, college. Little league trophy probably attic. Apple core, trash. You can do the rest.
(14) Mom: No buts. You choose the toys you want to donate, I'll drop them off at the Sunnyside.
(19) Mom: Like what are you going to do with these toys? Should we donate them to Sunnyside?
(21) Mom: Maybe sell them online.
(10) Molly: What kids?
(22) Andy: Mom, none is going to want those old toys. They are junk.
(8) Molly: 3 more days and it's mine.
(20) Andy: No.
(16) Toy: I get the Corvette.
(17) Mom: Andy, come on. You have to start making decisions.
(24) Andy: Whatever you say, mom.
(18) Andy: Like what?

AFTER VIEWING

Possible answer: Andy is going to college. *First* her sister asks him for his computer, stereo and video games. Her mother asks him to decide what to do with his things. He can put them in the trash, donate them or put them in the attic. He decides to put them in the attic, but by mistake they are put in the trash. *After that*, the toys escape. *Then* they enter a box in the car. *Finally* they decide to go to daycare.

GARFIELD: THE MOVIE
(GARFIELD: O FILME)

INFORMAÇÕES TÉCNICAS
Lançamento: 2004, EUA
Direção: Peter Hewitt
Vozes: Bill Murray (Garfield), Breckin Meyer (Jon), Jennifer Love Hewitt (Liz).
Gênero: Comédia

SINOPSE

A vida não poderia ser melhor para Garfield, o gato mais adorado do mundo. Afundado numa poltrona confortável em frente à TV, saboreando seu prato favorito, lasanha, e insultando o dono Jon, Garfield é o rei de seu universo. Jon leva Garfield para uma visita à bela veterinária Liz Wilson e ela lhe entrega uma criaturinha alegre e ofegante abanando o rabo, que representa tudo o que Garfield detesta: Odie, um adorável e não muito inteligente... cão. Pela primeira vez em suas sete vidas, o gato rabugento fica sem fala. Odie, que nem desconfia, persegue o próprio rabo até ficar tonto, choca-se contra as paredes e late sem motivo, encantando Jon, que o leva para casa.

TEACHING TIPS

Converse com os alunos a respeito dos diferentes gêneros de filmes. Explore com eles todos os gêneros (*science fiction*, *drama*, *comedy*, *action*, *adventure*, *epics/historical*, *musical*, *war*, *western* etc.). Peça aos alunos que digam seus gêneros preferidos e justifiquem. Dependendo do perfil da sua turma, introduza os nomes dos gêneros, mas a discussão pode ser feita na língua materna. Em seguida faça as perguntas do *Before viewing*.

No *Viewing*, leia as perguntas com os alunos, cubra a tela com papel e oriente-os para que ouçam a sequência com o objetivo de responder às perguntas oralmente. Os alunos podem tomar notas no espaço indicado. Em seguida retire o papel, peça que assistam à sequência do vídeo e respondam às mesmas perguntas por escrito, comparando-as com as respostas anteriores.

No *After viewing* oriente os alunos a usarem a atividade II como base para passar as sentenças para o passado e escrever o parágrafo. No trecho seguinte (*Viewing*) peça aos alunos que respondam às perguntas. Em seguida, cubra novamente a tela, passe a nova sequência (*Viewing, no picture*) e peça que coloquem as falas na ordem certa. Peça que troquem ideias sobre o que está acontecendo na cena e as anotem no local indicado. Mostre a cena e peça que confirmem suas ideias.

ANSWERS

BEFORE VIEWING

1. Comedy.
2. Open answer.

(00:00:36-00:04:34) ### VIEWING

I. Open answer.

II.

1. Garfield's house.
2. Garfield and Jon.
3. Jon is his caretaker.
4. They are waking up on a Monday morning. Garfield wakes Jon up by jumping on him. Jon has a shower and they have breakfast.

III.

(6) Jon hugs Garfield.
(2) The alarm goes off.
(7) Garfield jumps on Jon.
(3) Garfield says "I hate Mondays".
(8) Jon takes a shower.
(10) Garfield goes out.
(5) Garfield uncovers Jon.
(4) Garfield jumps on the bed.
(1) Garfield is snoring.
(9) They have breakfast.

AFTER VIEWING

Suggestion:
Yesterday Garfield woke up. He was snoring. It was Monday. He got out of bed and jumped on Jon's bed. He uncovered John. Jon hugged Garfield. Garfield was not happy. He jumped on top of Jon. Jon got up and took a shower. They had breakfast together.

(00:00:36-00:04:34) ### VIEWING

I.

1. Liver flavored.
2. Garfield switches their breakfast.
3. Every day.
4. He thinks it is dangerous. Bad things happen out there.

(00:10:27-00:13:05)

VIEWING (NO PICTURE)

I.

(5) Come on... let's go for a ride to some place you love. It always leaves you feeling pampered and refreshed.
(4) Love me, feed me and never leave me.
(1) Did you eat all the four boxes of Lasagna?
(6) Oh... I know... Chucky Cheese... Thank you. No... Wendy's...
(2) It's not my fault. They started it.
(7) There is nothing wrong with Garfield. He is just a happy, fat, lazy cat.
(3) What am I going to do with you?

II.

No picture	Picture
Open answers.	Garfield ate 4 boxes of lasagna. Jon puts him in the car. They go to the vet.

III.

1. Because he wants to see the Vet. He has a crush on her.
2. He has a crush on her.
3. She has never seen an owner so worried about his cat.
4. Since high school.
5. A dog.

THE TERMINAL
(O TERMINAL)

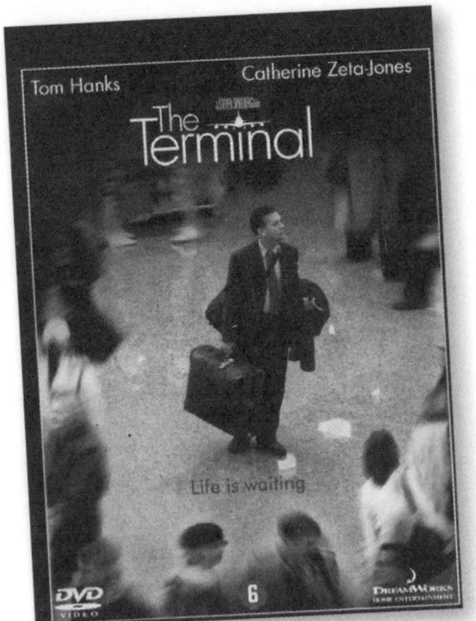

INFORMAÇÕES TÉCNICAS
Lançamento: 2004, EUA
Direção: Steven Spielberg
Elenco: Tom Hanks, Catherine Zeta-Jones, Stanley Tucci, Kenneth Choi
Gênero: Drama

SINOPSE

Viktor Navorski (Tom Hanks) é um cidadão da Europa Oriental que viaja rumo a Nova York justamente quando seu país sofre um golpe de estado, o que faz com que seu passaporte seja invalidado. Ao chegar ao aeroporto, Viktor não consegue autorização para entrar nos Estados Unidos. Sem poder retornar à sua terra natal, pois as fronteiras foram fechadas após o golpe, Viktor passa a improvisar seus dias e noites no próprio aeroporto, à espera de que a situação se resolva. Porém, com a situação se arrastando por meses, Viktor permanece no aeroporto e descobre o complexo mundo do terminal onde está preso.

TEACHING TIPS

Comece a aula conversando sobre viagens e para onde os alunos gostam de viajar. Pergunte qual o meio de transporte mais usado em suas viagens. Faça um levantamento sobre o que eles mais gostam de fazer nas viagens e o que mais lhes desagrada. Discuta com eles as vantagens e desvantagens dos vários meios de transporte. Observe que aqui é reforçada a formulação de perguntas relacionadas a aeroportos. Use também as perguntas do *Before viewing* para contextualizar.

Leia os itens do *Viewing* com os alunos. Peça que assistam à primeira cena e assinalem os itens que conseguiram ver. Peça que assistam à sequência novamente e escrevam as três perguntas feitas pelo policial da imigração. Leia as perguntas seguintes com os alunos e peça que respondam de acordo com o vídeo.

No *After viewing*, converse com os alunos sobre os preparativos necessários para uma viagem e utilize o modal should. Observe o perfil do seu grupo para ajustar seu discurso à realidade dele. Uma conversa com adolescentes será diferente de uma conversa com uma classe com perfil de executivos.

ANSWERS

BEFORE VIEWING

1. to **7.** Open answers.

8.

Free shop	How much does this cost? Can I help you, sir? Do you have ________?
Passport Control	How long are you staying? Can I see your passport, please? Business or pleasure?
Baggage Reclaim	Can I see your ticket? Can I see your baggage tag?
Customs	Anything to declare? Can you open your suitcase, please? Do you have any forbidden items?

(00:00:00-00:00:55) VIEWING

dogs; people; flags; benches; plants; doors; baggage belt; policemen; booths; names of cities

(00:01:00-00:01:25) VIEWING

1. Possible answers: What is the purpose of your visit? Business or pleasure? How long will you be staying in the United States? Can I see your return ticket, please?
2. Have students compare their answers to the chart.

(00:01:34-00:03:10) VIEWING

(3) Japanese people running.
(1) People arriving.
(5) Passport Control officer looks at his passport.
(2) The Director of Customs looking at the TV monitor.
(6) People taking their suitcases off the luggage belt.
(4) Mr. Navorski talking to the Passport Control officer.
(7) Mr. Navorski shaving.

(00:03:14-00:06:00) VIEWING

1. Possible answers: What exactly are you doing in the United States, Mr Navorski? Staying at the Ramada Inn? Do you know anyone in New York? Who? Mr. Navorski, I am gonna need to see your return ticket, please.
2. No.
3. Krakozhia.
4. There was a military coup.
5. Ramada Inn Hotel.

(00:08:46-00:10:00) VIEWING

1. A pager to contact them if necessary, food vouchers to buy food in the food court, 15 min prepaid calling card to call home, ID badge for identification.
2. America is closed.
3. Shop.

AFTER VIEWING

1. Open answer.
2. Open answer.
3. Suggestions:
You should pack your bag.
You should make sure you have all the necessary documents: ticket, passport, visa, health insurance etc.
You should have hotel reservations.
You should exchange your money for the correct currency.
You should have flight reservations.

THE SIXTH SENSE
(O SEXTO SENTIDO)

INFORMAÇÕES TÉCNICAS
Lançamento: 1999, EUA
Direção: M. Night Shyamalan
Elenco: Haley Joel Osment, Bruce Willis, Toni Collette, Olivia Williams
Gênero: Suspense

SINOPSE

O psicólogo infantil Malcolm Crowe (Bruce Willis) abraça com dedicação o caso de Cole Sear (Haley Joel Osment). O garoto de 8 anos tem dificuldades de entrosamento no colégio e vive paralisado de medo. Malcolm, por sua vez, busca se recuperar de um trauma sofrido anos antes, quando um de seus pacientes se suicidou na sua frente.

TEACHING TIPS

Essa atividade serve para reforçar o uso do tempo passado. Comece a aula contextualizando o tópico com os alunos. Pergunte se eles gostam desse gênero de filme antes de iniciar. Converse sobre os nossos cinco sentidos e quais eles acham que mais utilizam (olfato, audição, visão, tato e paladar). Pergunte se eles acreditam que possa existir outro sentido.

No primeiro *Viewing*, leia as perguntas com os alunos e mostre a sequência sem som. Peça que tomem nota de suas impressões. Em seguida passe a cena novamente, com som, peça que respondam às perguntas por escrito e comparem suas ideias com a atividade anterior. Levante hipóteses com eles sobre a quinta pergunta.

Contextualize a cena seguinte usando as perguntas do *Before viewing* e em seguida peça que respondam as perguntas.

Siga as instruções e observe que, no *After viewing*, os alunos deverão recontar essa história ou alguma similar empregando o tempo passado.

ANSWERS

BEFORE VIEWING

1. Open answer.
2. Open answer.
3. We have 5 senses: sight, hearing, taste, touch and smell.
4. Open answer.
5. Open answer.

SICK GIRL SCENE (01:22:00-01:26:36) I. VIEWING (NO SOUND)

Open answers.

II. VIEWING (WITH SOUND)

1. The boy and a man.
2. Open answer.
3. She was poisoned.
4. Her mother.
5. Someone told him.

SECRET SCENE (00:50:14-00:51:30) → BEFORE VIEWING

Open answers.

→ VIEWING

1. He sees dead people.
2. The dead girl told him.

THE GAME SCENE (00:20:40-00:26:00) → VIEWING

(1) Wanna sit?
(10) How do you draw now?
(7) Your dad gave you that watch as a present just before he went away...
(5) You're worried that if she said you told him things...
(2) Don't feel like talking today?
(3) Wanna play a game?
(8) You keep pretty quiet at school but you are a good student...
(6) You have a secret but you don't want to tell me.
(9) You saw that on TV...
(4) When your mum and dad were first divorced your mum went to see a doctor like me and he did not help her.

LAST SCENE (01:31:06-01:36:00) → VIEWING

hurt; quiet, important; secrets; accident; lady; see; window; Ghosts; talk; freak; face; minute; visit; dance, fight.

→ AFTER VIEWING

Open answer.

THE DEVIL WEARS PRADA

(O DIABO VESTE PRADA)

INFORMAÇÕES TÉCNICAS
Lançamento: 2006, EUA
Direção: David Frankel
Elenco: Meryl Streep, Anne Hathaway, Emily Blunt, Stanley Tucci, Gisele Bundchen, Adrian Grenier, Simon Baker
Gênero: Comédia romântica

SINOPSE

Com estilo interiorano e inocente, Andy Sachs (Anne Hathaway) chega a Nova York. Recém-formada em jornalismo, ela se muda para a Big Apple com seu namorado Nate e sai em busca de um emprego. Finalmente consegue uma entrevista na badalada revista de moda *Runway Magazine*, comandada pela impetuosa e obcecada editora Miranda Priestly (Meryl Streep). Mesmo sem nunca ter ouvido falar da revista ou da famosa editora, ela consegue o emprego, em razão de seu "excelente currículo e de seu discurso sobre a ética de trabalho", como afirmado pela própria Miranda Priestly. Seu estilo, entretanto, é motivo de piada entre os novos colegas de trabalho. Determinada a seguir em frente com o desafio, Andy muda seu visual e se torna uma *workaholic* nas mãos de sua abominável chefe.

TEACHING TIPS

Essa atividade pode ser usada para reforçar o vocabulário relacionado a vestuário e a adjetivos, descrevendo personalidades e sentimentos. Observar que cada sequência tem uma atividade de *Before viewing* importante para levantar o conhecimento prévio dos alunos. Nas atividades em que os alunos necessitarão dar opiniões, introduzir as estruturas: *In my opinion, I believe that, I think that, In my point of view*. O *After viewing* pode ser usado como *homework*. Sugira que os alunos assistam ao filme todo em casa.

ANSWERS

BEFORE VIEWING

1. Open answer.
2. We should wear formal clothes for a job interview.

(00:00:30–00:03:25) **VIEWING**

I.

dresses; skirts; bra; panties; socks; blouses; coats; handbags; earrings; lipstick; mascara; cosmetics; eye shadow; scarfs; high heeled shoes; gloves; long overcoats; pullover; stockings; boots; caps; fur coat

II.

1. New York.
2. It's winter. It's cold.
3. She takes the subway.
4. No, she's not.
5. She should wear a dress, high heeled shoes, an elegant overcoat and her hair should be neatly combed.

ANSWERS

BEFORE VIEWING

1. You usually feel nervous and anxious before a job interview.
2. You should research about the company you are going to visit and about the person you are going to talk to.

CHAPTER 2 (00:03:25–00:04:35) ### VIEWING

1. At the headquarters of a big company.
2. Nervous.
3. It's a publishing company.
4. Editor in chief.
5. Ironic, stressed.
6. No. She is a journalist.

BEFORE VIEWING

I.

POSITIVE	NEGATIVE
hard-working, humorous, critical, polite, imaginative, ambitious, calm, experienced, supportive, decisive, generous, sociable, considerate, well-organized, diplomatic, punctual, respectful, competent, confident, trustful, helpful	snobbish, conceited, stressed, bossy, ironic, rude, intimidating, incompetent, dishonest

II. Possible answers: An ideal boss should be open minded, a leader, sensitive towards his/her employees in the working environment, respectful, competent, helpful and trustful. Other adjectives that can be used to describe an ideal boss: hard-working, humorous, critical, polite, imaginative, ambitious, tidy, calm, experienced, supportive, decisive, generous, sociable, considerate, well-organized, diplomatic, punctual.

CHAPTER 3 (00:04:35–00:06:35) ### VIEWING

1. She's bossy, snobbish, not respectful, not generous.
2. Everybody seems afraid of her.
3. Yes, she does.
4. She asks: *Who are you? What are you doing here?*
5. *My name is Andy Sachs. I recently graduated from Northwestern University. I think I could do a good job as your assistant.*

CHAPTER 13 (00:35:45-00:36:27) ### VIEWING

1. She looks quite different.
2. *Before* she was a girl who dressed herself without taking fashion into consideration. She had no style and her hair was not well cut. *After* she became a fashionable girl.

AFTER VIEWING

Open answer.

JUNO

INFORMAÇÕES TÉCNICAS
Lançamento: 2007, EUA
Direção: James Reitman
Elenco: Ellen Page, Michael Cera, Jennifer Gamer
Gênero: Comédia romântica

SINOPSE

O filme mostra situações de uma menina de 16 anos chamada Juno, que engravida de seu companheiro de classe Bleeker e decide não fazer um aborto. Com a ajuda do pai, da madrasta e da melhor amiga Lea, a jovem adolescente procura o casal "perfeito" para criar seu filho e encara situações delicadas e incomuns para sua maturidade.

TEACHING TIPS

Essa atividade pode ser realizada por adolescentes ou adultos, pois trata de um tema polêmico: gravidez na adolescência. As questões do *Before viewing* podem ser respondidas na língua materna, de acordo com o nível linguístico dos alunos. Se optar pela língua-alvo, oriente os alunos a usarem a linguagem adequada para dar opiniões: *I think..., In my opinion..., I guess...* e também estimule-os a usar *I agree, I don't agree, I completely agree, I totally disagree, I understand your point of view but...* para concordar ou discordar.

Faça um levantamento sobre os adjetivos que eles conhecem relacionados a *feelings* e escreva-os na lousa antes do primeiro *Viewing*. Na cena seguinte, coloque a sequência sem som e peça que os alunos imaginem o que está acontecendo. Faça isso em pares. Em seguida peça que assistam novamente à sequência e primeiramente completem e depois ordenem as sentenças.

No *After viewing* coloque os alunos em pares para discutirem a questão antes de escreverem.

ANSWERS

BEFORE VIEWING

Open answers.

(00:21:22-00:25:10) VIEWING

I.

Juno feels: embarrassed; afraid; confused; determined
Her dad is: surprised; supportive
Her step mother is: calm; concerned
Lea, her best friend, is: cooperative; helpful; friendly; encouraging

II.

to give the child to adoption; she's not ready to be a mother

(00:54:05-00:57:13) ➡ VIEWING

I.

Open answer.

II.

Juno: ... the mall today
Vanessa: ... shopping ...
Juno: ... her
Vanessa: ... okay
Vanessa: ... are ... feeling
Juno: ... Everything ...
Vanessa: ... incredible

III.

(2) What?
(5) Are you kidding? Go on.
(7) I'm a legend. They call me the cautionary whale.
(11) Can you hear me, baby? Sweet angel?
(12) I felt it. Oh, God. That was magical.
(1) Oh, God.
(8) I can't feel anything. It's not moving for me.
(4) Could I feel it?
(10) Hi, baby. It's me. It's Vanessa. I can't wait to meet you.
(3) Kicking away.
(9) You should try talking to it because supposedly they can hear you even though it's like 10,000 leagues under the sea.
(6) At school everyone is just grabbing my belly all the time. It's crazy!
(13) Thank you. Thank you.

➡ AFTER VIEWING

Suggestions:
You should see a doctor.
You should speak to your parents.
You should speak to your friends.
You should speak to your boyfriend/girlfriend.
You should make sure you use protection.

AVATAR

INFORMAÇÕES TÉCNICAS
Lançamento: 2009, EUA, Inglaterra
Direção: James Cameron
Elenco: Sam Worthington, Sigourney Weaver, Michelle Rodriguez, Zoe Saldana, Giovanni Ribisi, Joel Moore
Gênero: Ação

SINOPSE

Avatar é um filme americano de ficção científica. A história se passa no ano 2154 e é baseada em um conflito em Pandora, uma das luas de Polifemo, um dos três planetas gasosos fictícios que orbitam o sistema Alpha Centauri. Em Pandora, os colonizadores humanos e os Na'vi, nativos humanoides, entram em guerra pelos recursos do planeta e pela continuação da existência da espécie nativa. O título do filme refere-se aos corpos Na'vi-humanos híbridos, criados por um grupo de cientistas por meio de engenharia genética para interagir com os nativos de Pandora.

TEACHING TIPS

Inicie a aula com as perguntas do *Before viewing*. Se seus alunos forem adultos, em vez de usar as primeiras perguntas sobre Ciências, comece com a terceira pergunta. Em seguida pergunte quais filmes de ficção científica eles já assistiram. Questione se eles acreditam que possa existir vida em outros planetas e como seria essa vida. Contextualize o assunto.

Leia com eles as perguntas no quadro do *Viewing* antes de assistirem ao vídeo. Peça que tomem nota no quadro enquanto assistem, respondam e comparem as respostas em pares ao terminar. Faça as questões do *After viewing* com a classe toda.

No segundo *Before viewing* contextualize o assunto perguntando aos alunos se eles acreditam que os animais e as plantas têm alguma forma de ligação com os seres humanos. Leia a pergunta e peça que respondam oralmente. Mostre a cena sem som. Peça que descrevam a cena com suas próprias palavras usando os marcadores de sequência *first, then, after and finally*. Oriente que compartilhem suas respostas com um colega. Mostre novamente com som para que respondam às perguntas seguintes.

A terceira sequência pode ajudar os alunos a refletirem sobre sua própria cultura, comparando-a com a cultura de outros povos. Siga as instruções e troque ideias com os alunos a respeito desse assunto. Peça que pensem em cerimônias que têm um real significado para eles e a razão disso. Peça que pensem em outras culturas e nas cerimônias importantes para elas. Explore bem esse tópico. Ao descrever uma cerimônia, eles podem repensar o que os rituais representam em uma sociedade.

ANSWERS

BEFORE VIEWING

Open answers.

(00:09:35-00:11:48) ### VIEWING

He is talking into a video log to document his feelings and observations about the mission he is about to be part of.
Because it is part of Science to observe everything and according to one of the men it will keep him sane for the next 6 years.
Every driver is matched with an Avatar so their nervous systems are in tune.
Good Science is good observation.
She is a legend. She is the head of the Avatar program and she wrote the book on Pandora Botany.
No, she does not. She wants Jake's brother.
The Na'vi language.
They both speak the language. Norm is still learning.
He died.

AFTER VIEWING

Open answers.

(01:04:00-01:04:15) ### BEFORE VIEWING

Open answer.

VIEWING (NO SOUND)

Open answer.

VIEWING (WITH SOUND)

1. They believe there is a network of energy that flows through the living things and that all energy is only borrowed and that one day we have to give it back.
2. Open answer.

(01:18:33-01:21:23) ### BEFORE VIEWING

Suggestions:
Wedding, baptism, circumcision, wedding anniversary, bar mitzvah, birthday etc.

VIEWING

1. He is contemplative.
2. Yes, he has.
3. He feels he has not finished the job yet. He wants to be completely accepted by the Na'vi.
4. To have the movements of his legs back.
5. Yes, he was.
6. Possible answer: Jake has his face painted by a Na'vi. He is then taken to the chief of the tribe who welcomes him to their people. The people next to Jake place their hands on his shoulder and all the other Na'vis place their hands on the person in front of them, connecting them all to Jake.
7. Blue, tall, long nose, long arms, intuitive. (Take other suggestions as answers too.)
8. The Na'vi say that every person is born twice. The second time is when you earn your place among the people forever.

AFTER VIEWING

Open answers.

HITCH
(HITCH – CONSELHEIRO AMOROSO)

SINOPSE

Nessa sofisticada comédia romântica, Alex "Hitch" Hitchens (Will Smith) é um lendário "doutor do amor" residente em Nova York, que, por uma pequena taxa, já ajudou inúmeros homens a conquistar as mulheres de seus sonhos.

Enquanto atua como conselheiro sentimental para Albert (Kevin James), um humilde e meigo contador que caiu de amores pela charmosa socialite Allegra Cole (Amber Valletta), Hitch finalmente conhece aquela que imagina ser a sua própria cara-metade. Isso acontece quando encontra a gloriosa e espertíssima Sara Melas (Eva Mendes), uma repórter que escreve para uma coluna de fofocas e anda no encalço de Allegra, seguindo cada um de seus passos.

INFORMAÇÕES TÉCNICAS
Lançamento: 2005, EUA
Direção: Andy Tennant
Elenco: Will Smith, Eva Mendes, Kevin James, Amber Valletta, Michael Rapaport e Adam Arkin
Gênero: Comédia

TEACHING TIPS

Observe o perfil do seu grupo ao escolher essa atividade. Se forem adolescentes, pergunte como eles iniciam um relacionamento e convidam pessoas para sair. Se forem adultos comprometidos, pergunte como eles conheceram seus pares e se eles acham que essa prática de relacionamento mudou. Use essa atividade para reforçar o uso das descrições de lugares, acontecimentos e pessoas. No segundo *Viewing*, reforce o uso dos advérbios de frequência. Observe que o *Viewing* da *Dancing scene* deve ser feito sem som. No *After viewing*, enfatize o uso do imperativo.

ANSWERS

BEFORE VIEWING

Open answers.

(00:15:21-00:18:23) VIEWING

1. In the office.
2. Computer, coffee mug, pen, paper.
3. A little overweight, short hair, wears glasses.
4. Clumsy and insecure.
5. Albert and Hitch.
6. He helps people get into a relationship.
7. You swing for the fence.
8. Albert needs Hitch to help him get into a relationship.
9. Open answer.

(00:20:35-00:25:53) ➡ VIEWING

I.

1. Usually, never.
People don't **usually** talk to me like that, ok?
Let me rephrase that people **never** talk to me like that.
2. Always, rarely, sometimes, often.

II.

IN THE MEETING ROOM

1. Allegra – CEO/ Albert – Financial advisor.
2. There is a big table, there are many people and there are many chairs.
3. Allegra's wish to invest in another area.
4. He took Allegra's side and disagreed with his boss.
5. He quit his job.
6. I quit.

IN ALBERT'S OFFICE

7. Albert's behavior in the meeting room.
8. Facial expressions, body posture.
9. Before: frustrated, angry and disappointed. After: amazed, happy.
10. She asked him if they could meet one day during that week to discuss financial issues.

DANCING SCENE (00:49:33-00:50:50) ➡ BEFORE VIEWING

Open answers.

➡ VIEWING

1. Albert is dancing. He describes his movements and Hitch does not like what he sees. Hitch teaches Albert how to dance his way.
2. Start the fire; get the feet going; make the pizza.
3. No. He does not approve of Albert's dancing.

➡ AFTER VIEWING

1. Open answer.
2. Suggestions: always dress decently, never talk too much, arrive on time, don't be rude, be polite, never be late, don't talk on the cell phone, don't drink too much, don't talk about past relationships etc.

THE SHAWSHANK REDEMPTION
(UM SONHO DE LIBERDADE)

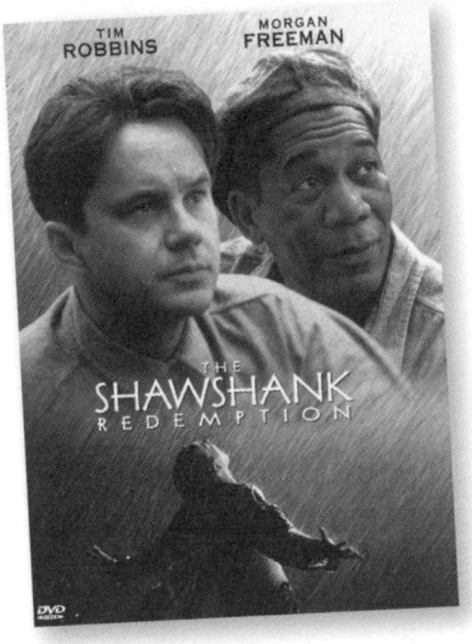

INFORMAÇÕES TÉCNICAS
Lançamento: 1994, EUA
Direção: Frank Darabont
Elenco: Tim Robbins, Morgan Freeman, Bob Gunton, William Sadler
Gênero: Drama

SINOPSE

Em 1946, Andy Dufresne (Tim Robbins), um jovem e bem-sucedido banqueiro, tem a sua vida radicalmente modificada quando mandado para uma penitenciária para cumprir prisão perpétua por ter assassinado sua mulher e o amante dela. No presídio, faz amizade com Ellis Boyd Redding (Morgan Freeman), um prisioneiro que cumpre pena há 20 anos e controla o mercado negro do presídio.

TEACHING TIPS

Comece a aula discutindo sobre a política de carceragem no Brasil. Pergunte aos alunos o que eles sabem a respeito e se podem opinar sobre como melhorá-la. Leve em conta a idade de seus alunos para saber o quanto pode aprofundar esse assunto. Faça as perguntas do *Before viewing*.

No primeiro *Viewing* mostre a cena sem som e peça que os alunos criem um diálogo entre as personagens. Peça que compartilhem o diálogo em pares. Em seguida, mostre a cena com o som e peça que ordenem as falas. Oriente-os para que comparem o diálogo elaborado por eles com o do filme.

No segundo *Viewing* leia as perguntas com os alunos antes de assistir à cena. Peça que respondam em pares.

No terceiro *Viewing* os alunos devem completar as sentenças de acordo com a cena. Se seus alunos já aprenderam o discurso indireto, faça a atividade seguinte.

Use a atividade do *After viewing* para aprofundar o uso de *wish*.

ANSWERS

BEFORE VIEWING

1. Depressing, dirty, scary, sad, and dangerous. (Accept other answers.)
2. Dangerous people, murderers, robbers, rapists, white collar thieves.
3. For raping, for murdering, for stealing cars, for moral issues, for lying, for hijacking, for kidnapping, for blackmailing.
4. Using their external contacts, through visitors, paying off the guards.
5. Open answer.

(00:06:22-00:07:20)

VIEWING (NO SOUND)

Open answers.

VIEWING (WITH SOUND)

(4) You feel you have been rehabilitated?
(1) Sit.
(3) Yes, sir.
(5) Oh, yes sir. Absolutely sir. I mean I have learnt my lesson.
(6) I can honestly say I am a changed man, I am no longer a danger to society. That's God's honest truth.
(2) We see by your file you have served 20 years of a life sentence.

(00:07:20-00:13:45) VIEWING

1. Cigarettes, drinks, posters, anything within reason.
2. A poster of Rita Hayworth.
3. 1947.
4. Murdering his wife and her lover.
5. Vice-president of a Portland bank.
6. Not really. He thought a stiff breeze would knock him over.
7. Mr. Norton.
8. Discipline and the Bible.
9. Open answer.

(02:12:53-02:15:45) VIEWING

I.

1. gotten out
2. good man; on wheels
3. keep an eye out for you
4. hope; dies; letter

II.

Open answer.

AFTER VIEWING

I.

1. Red wishes Andy were there.
2. Red wishes the prisoners would stop fighting.
3. Andy wishes he had more money.
4. Red wishes he hadn't fought with an intern the night before.
5. Red wishes he had some cigarettes.

II.

Open answer.

PRETTY WOMAN
(UMA LINDA MULHER)

INFORMAÇÕES TÉCNICAS
Lançamento: 1990, EUA
Direção: Garry Marshall
Elenco: Richard Gere e Julia Roberts
Gênero: Romance

SINOPSE

Magnata (Richard Gere) pede ajuda a uma prostituta (Julia Roberts) do Hollywood Boulevard e a contrata por uma semana. Nesse período, ela se transforma em uma elegante jovem para poder acompanhá-lo em seus compromissos sociais. No final os dois se envolvem emocionalmente.

TEACHING TIPS

Esse filme trata do relacionamento entre um homem e uma prostituta. Verifique o perfil do seu grupo antes de realizar essa atividade, para ter certeza de que tenham maturidade para lidar com o assunto.

No *Before viewing* pergunte se alguém já assistiu a esse filme. Se eles ainda não assistiram ao filme, levante hipóteses com os alunos sobre o título. Leia com os alunos as perguntas do *Viewing* antes de mostrar o filme. Oriente que verifiquem as respostas em pares.

No segundo *Before viewing* leia a pergunta e troque ideias com os alunos a respeito desse tópico. No segundo *Viewing*, peça que completem a tabela com as características de cada personagem. Em seguida peça que respondam as perguntas.

No terceiro *Before viewing* compartilhe ideias sobre vestuário adequado para cada ocasião. Converse com os alunos sobre a importância de se vestir adequadamente para cada situação. Em seguida, mostre a cena e faça a atividade de *Viewing*.

No *After viewing*, relembre os alunos do uso do modal *should/ shouldn't*.

ANSWERS

BEFORE VIEWING
Open answer.

(01:39:00-01:45:00) VIEWING

1. They are partners. They work together.
2. They are closing a business.
3. Closes the curtains, offers some coffee.
4. I no longer wish to buy your company and tear it apart. But I don't want anyone else to either. And it is still extremely vulnerable. So I find myself in unfamiliar territory. I wanna help you.
5. I am proud of you.
6.

Blow off
Hooker, whore
How to hit a woman

7. Open answer.

(00:31:11-00:36:19) BEFORE VIEWING

Open answer.

VIEWING

1.

	Personality characteristics	Physical characteristics
Edward	Secure, intelligent, sophisticated, charming, successful businessman, hard working, lonely. (Accept other possibilities.)	Handsome, grey hair, medium height, medium weight.
Vivian	Naive, not smart, charming, insecure, childish. (Accept other possibilities.)	Beautiful, long brown hair, brown eyes, thin, tall.

2. There are a few chairs here.
3. He is a successful businessman who buys companies that are in financial difficulties.
4. She is a hooker.
5. Stealing cars and selling them for parts.
6. For Vivian to be his companion for the week.
7. U$ 3000,00.

SHOPPING SCENE (00:40:18-00:41:20) BEFORE VIEWING

Open answers.

VIEWING

1. Badly. They did not want her in the shop.
2. Open answer.
3. To show respect to the people who you are with, to follow a protocol. (Accept other answers.)
4. a. F; b. T; c. T; d. F; e. F.

AFTER VIEWING

Suggestions: You should behave adequately, you shouldn't eat with your mouth open, you should always put your napkin on your lap, you should not put your elbow on the table.

HOW TO LOSE A GUY IN 10 DAYS
(COMO PERDER UM HOMEM EM 10 DIAS)

INFORMAÇÕES TÉCNICAS
Lançamento: 2003, EUA, Alemanha
Direção: Donald Petrie
Elenco: Kate Hudson, Matthew McConaughey
Gênero: Comédia romântica

SINOPSE

Andie Anderson (Kate Hudson) é jornalista da revista *Composure*. Ela deve escrever um artigo sobre "Como perder um homem em 10 dias". Para poder escrever de forma mais realista, ela decide namorar um rapaz e fazer tudo de errado que as mulheres tendem a fazer em um relacionamento. Ao mesmo tempo, o executivo de *marketing* Benjamin Barry (Matthew McConaughey) diz a seu chefe que ele pode fazer qualquer mulher se apaixonar por ele em 10 dias.

TEACHING TIPS

É importante contextualizar usando as perguntas iniciais. Use a língua-alvo todo o tempo. Leia as perguntas com os alunos antes de colocar o vídeo, para que eles assistam tendo um objetivo claro. Organize a classe em pares e peça que respondam às questões do *Before viewing*. Apresente o vocabulário da questão 2 e peça que reflitam sobre seu próprio relacionamento com as pessoas. Pode ser interessante que os pares sejam formados por pessoas de sexos opostos.

Leia as perguntas do *Viewing* com os alunos para que as respondam objetivamente. Peça que façam a atividade de verdadeiro ou falso, corrigindo as sentenças falsas. A última atividade (*After viewing*) pode ser feita como *homework*. Obs.: O uso de dicionário pode ser necessário para a segunda questão.

ANSWERS

BEFORE VIEWING

1. Open answers.
2. Suggestions:

Dos	Don'ts
Be cool, fun, smart, beautiful/ handsome, take him/her to concerts, get along fine with his/her parents, go to places both like, be charming, look good all the time, be polite.	Be clingy, act needy, whiny, use baby talk, talk about babies, about marriage, be obsessed about old boyfriends, appear on the boys'/girls' night, prepare "yummy" snacks, ask him/her not to smoke, disturb the games, talk to his/her mother behind his/her back, act insane.

CHAPTER 13 → VIEWING

(GIRLS TALKING – 00:59:54-01:00:50)

I.

1. They suggested Andie to be clingy, needy, whiny, use baby talk, talk about old boyfriends.
2. Yes, she has already done everything.
3. They tell her to ruin the boys' night.

(THE BOYS NIGHT – 01:00:50-01:06:30).

II.

1. They are playing poker, smoking cigars, eating pizza, drinking bear and talking about Ben's girlfriend.
2. Francesco, the super, made a copy for her.
3. She was not being expected. She puts the dog on the table. She interrupts their game. She brought some "yummy" snacks – cucumber sandwiches. She treats them like babies. She starts coughing and asks them to stop smoking. She tells the cards. She makes Ben blow his nose. She complains about the "love fern". She acts insane.
4. Open answer.
5.
a. F. They are playing poker.
b. T.
c. F. The fern is dry and dead.
d. F Andie is acting insane.
e. T.
f. F. Ben's dog got nervous and began barking.

→ AFTER VIEWING

Open answers.

INGLORIOUS BASTERDS
(BASTARDOS INGLÓRIOS)

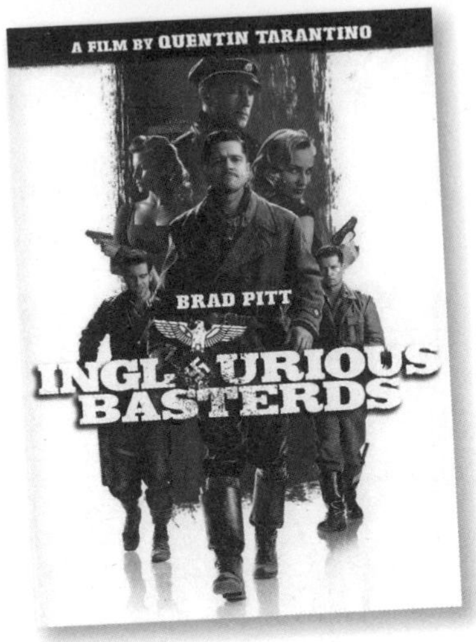

INFORMAÇÕES TÉCNICAS
Lançamento: 2009, EUA, Alemanha
Direção: Quentin Tarantino
Elenco: Brad Pitt, Melanie Laurent, Christopher Waltz
Gênero: Guerra, drama

SINOPSE

No primeiro ano da ocupação da França pela Alemanha, Shosanna Dreyfus testemunha a execução de sua família pelas mãos do coronel nazista Hans Landa (Christopher Waltz). Shosanna escapa por pouco e parte para Paris, onde assume uma identidade falsa e se torna proprietária de um cinema. Em outro lugar da Europa, o tenente Aldo Raine (Brad Pitt) organiza um grupo de soldados americanos judeus para praticarem atos violentos de vingança. Posteriormente chamados pelo inimigo de "Os Bastardos", o esquadrão de Raine se une à atriz alemã Bridget von Hammersmark em uma missão para derrubar os líderes do Terceiro Reich. O destino conspira para que os caminhos de todos se cruzem em um cinema, onde Shosanna pretende colocar em prática seu próprio plano de vingança.

TEACHING TIPS

É importante contextualizar o tópico por meio das primeiras perguntas. Se a atividade for usada para turmas do Ensino Fundamental 2 ou do Ensino Médio, é aconselhável que ela seja feita logo após o tema ter sido discutido em História. Se necessário, peça que seus alunos leiam sobre a Segunda Guerra Mundial com antecedência. Há um *link* abaixo com uma sugestão de leitura. Use a língua-alvo, porém, se sentir necessidade, utilize a língua materna para contextualizar e fazer o levantamento prévio do conhecimento dos alunos. As perguntas devem ser sempre lidas antes de assistirem ao vídeo, para que tenham bem claro os objetivos a serem alcançados. No *Viewing* peça que os alunos prestem atenção ao contexto em que as palavras e as expressões estão inseridas para que possam deduzir o significado. Oriente que façam em pares para que haja interação. A atividade seguinte reforça o uso das *If clauses*. Mostre a sequência novamente para que façam o exercício. No *After viewing* oriente-os a usarem frases como *I believe..., I think..., on the other hand..., I guess, I agree, I don't agree* etc. Sugira que assistam ao filme em casa para que na aula seguinte possam confirmar suas hipóteses.

Para ler sobre a Segunda Guerra Mundial: <http://www.bbc.co.uk/history/worldwars/wwtwo/ww2_summary_01.shtml>. Acesso em: 04/10/2011.

ANSWERS

BEFORE VIEWING

1. Open answer.
2. It began in 1939 and ended in 1945.
3. 61 million people died. The Allies won the war.
4. Allies and Axis.
5. France was occupied by the Germans.
6. They were the German leaders during the II World War.

CHAPTER 23 (02:03:35-02:10:24) **VIEWING**

I.

1.
Aldo: The apache.
Hans Landa: Jew hunter.
Utivich: Little man.

2. No, he doesn't agree. He says he's a good detective and worked for the Nazis finding people and some of them were Jews.

3. No, he didn't. Yes, he was really surprised.

II.

1. kindness that makes you forgive someone
2. unable to move, fixed
3. something easy to remember
4. damaged
5. to stop fighting and accept defeat

III.

(1) someone is experiencing what they used to make others experience, normally negative things
(5) acted illegally
(4) make an arrangement, an agreement
(2) receive what you deserve
(6) to summarize
(3) proceeding, operating

IV.

1. would; show
2. end
3. have
4. would; say

V.

He wants to make a deal with a general from OSS to end the war that night. The 4 German leaders would be killed and the war would be over.

AFTER VIEWING

Open answer.

FRIENDS - SEASON 4 - EPISODE 12

THE ONE WITH THE EMBRYOS

THE ROOMMATE GAME

INFORMAÇÕES TÉCNICAS
Lançamento: 1994, EUA
Criadores: Marta Kauffman, David Crane e Kevin S. Bright
Produtores: Kevin S. Bright, Marta Kauffman, David Crane, Shana Goldberg-Meehan e Scott Silveri
Elenco: Jennifer Aniston (Rachel Green), Courteney Cox Arquette (Monica Geller), Lisa Kudrow (Phoebe Buffay), Matt Le Blanc (Joey Tribbiani), David Schwimmer (Ross Geller), Matthew Perry (Chandler Bing)
Gênero: Comédia

SINOPSE

Friends, um clássico seriado de humor que contou com 10 temporadas (1994-2004), girava em torno de um grupo de seis amigos inseparáveis que viviam na área de Manhattan, na cidade de New York. Possui muitos fãs pelo mundo inteiro, pois todos que assistem conseguem se identificar com algum personagem e não se cansam de rir, seja com a mimada e bela Rachel; a sistêmica e cheia de manias Mônica; a divertida, desafinada e louca Phoebe; o mais lento, Joey; o divertido e reprimido, Chandler; e, por fim, o inteligente e cheio de decepções amorosas, Ross. Embora o tópico desse episódio seja a fertilização in vitro que Phoebe fará, o foco principal é o jogo de perguntas e respostas das personagens.

TEACHING TIPS

Antes de começar, converse sobre o seriado com o grupo. Pergunte se o conhecem e se gostam. Introduza a ideia de dividir um apartamento com amigos. Dependendo do perfil (adolescentes ou adultos), faça perguntas relevantes à idade. Se forem adolescentes, você pode sugerir a ideia de serem colegas de quarto em um acampamento. Se forem adultos, pergunte se moraram em uma república quando fizeram faculdade. Coloque-os em pares e peça que discutam as vantagens e desvantagens de compartilhar o mesmo espaço.

Antes de assistirem à sequência, peça que leiam as perguntas de 1 a 8 para você se certificar de que não há dúvidas. Mostre a sequência até que essas oito perguntas possam ser respondidas. Na nona questão oriente os alunos a fazerem uma lista de 10 itens que podem ser comprados em um supermercado. Peça que compartilhem as listas. Em seguida os alunos devem ler as demais perguntas, assistir à sequência novamente e responder em pares. Na atividade do *After viewing* os alunos farão um jogo de perguntas e respostas. Divida a classe em times. Cada time deverá formular cinco perguntas de conhecimentos gerais. Eles irão fazer suas perguntas ao adversário. Se o adversário acertar a resposta, o time faz um ponto. Jogue com seus alunos pelo tempo que eles estiverem entretidos. Eles podem formular novas perguntas. É uma ótima oportunidade para reforçar o uso de perguntas e respostas em inglês.

ANSWERS

BEFORE VIEWING

Open answers.

(00:00:00-00:02:50) ### VIEWING

1. Because Joey says he knows that that day is her laundry day and that she is wearing her old lady's underpants.
2. Old lady's underpants.
3. Open answer.
4. Five items.
5. cookies; chips; yogurt; soda
6. Scotch tape.
7. 10 bucks.
8. Because Joey and Chandler used up all the scotch tape the night before making funny faces.
9. Open answers.
10. 100 bucks
11. A game answering personal questions.
12. 100 bucks
13. 10 questions.
14. Fears and pet peeves, ancient History, Literature and it's all relative.
15. Stone, paper, scissors; toss a coin and numbers. They toss a coin.
16. Do you wanna bet?; So not true!; You're good.; So not impressed.; Fork it over.; Deal!

AFTER VIEWING

Group activity to answer orally.

INVICTUS

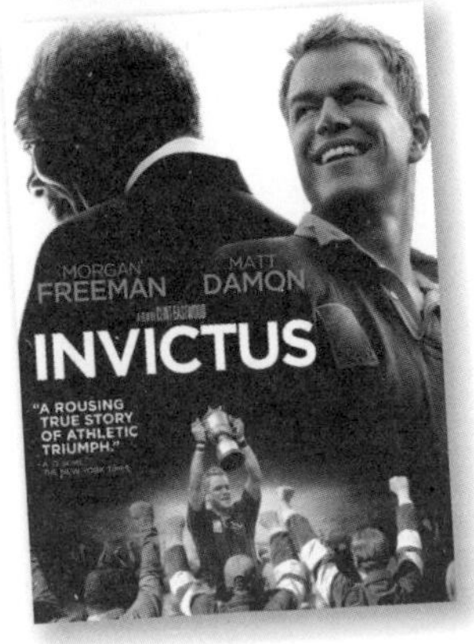

INFORMAÇÕES TÉCNICAS
Lançamento: 2009, EUA
Direção: Clint Eastwood
Elenco: Matt Damon, Morgan Freeman
Gênero: Drama

SINOPSE

Invictus nos traz a inspiradora história de como Nelson Mandela (Morgan Freeman) uniu forças com o capitão da equipe de rúgbi da África do Sul, Francois Pienaar (Matt Damon), para ajudar a unir a nação. Recém-eleito, o presidente Mandela sabe que seu país permanece dividido racial e economicamente após o fim do *apartheid*. Acreditando ser capaz de unificar a população por meio da linguagem universal do esporte, Mandela apoia o desacreditado time da África do Sul na Copa Mundial de Rúgbi de 1995, que faz uma incrível campanha até as finais.

TEACHING TIPS

Observe que as atividades de *Before viewing* são importantes para levantar o conhecimento prévio dos alunos.

As atividades podem ser feitas em duas ou até três aulas, ou você pode aplicar uma parte delas somente, dependendo do grupo. O *Before viewing* e os dois primeiros *Viewings* podem ser usados separadamente, especialmente com grupos que já tenham estudado o *apartheid*. Em uma segunda aula, a sequência de questões sobre liderança e esporte pode ser abordada. O poema pode ser utilizado em uma aula sobre literatura, e outros detalhes podem ser explorados. Outra possibilidade para as atividades de *Viewing* é que os próprios alunos formulem as perguntas após assistir à sequência. Em seguida, eles deverão fazer as perguntas para seus pares. O *After viewing* deve se feito fora da sala de aula. Peça que os alunos assistam ao filme em casa, com sua família, discutam as perguntas e as respondam.

Curiosidade: O hino sul-africano Nkosi sikelef' iAfrika (God bless Africa) inclui cinco das onze línguas oficiais da África do Sul e combina dois hinos: o do *apartheid* e o hino popular do Congresso Nacional Africano.

ANSWERS

BEFORE VIEWING

1. Apartheid refers to the policy of strict racial segregation and political and economic discrimination against non-whites practiced in the Republic of South Africa.
2. He was a South African president (1994-1999) and Black political leader imprisoned for nearly 30 years for his antiapartheid activities. Released in 1990, he led the African National Congress (ANC) in negotiating an end to apartheid. In 1993 he shared the Nobel Peace Prize. His former wife, Winnie (born in 1936), also played a key role as a leader of the ANC.

CHAPTER 1 (00:00:58-00:02:11) ➡ VIEWING

1. Two groups of teenagers: black and white teens playing soccer in quite different conditions – a little example of what apartheid was in South Africa.
2. In this context it means "to become worse in quality".

(00:02:11-00:04:20) ➡ VIEWING

1. Sunday, February 11th, 1990.
2. His release has triggered a struggle between the ANC and their black rivals. South Africa appears to be on the verge of (about to experience) a civil war.
3. Mandela says: "Take your knives and your guns and your pangas (large knives) and throw them into the sea."
4. For the first time they were free to cast their vote (to vote) alongside whites.
5. never again; beautiful land; oppression; indignity; the world; contemptible/worthless people.

(00:45:39-00:51:16) ➡ BEFORE VIEWING

Open answers. Some words that may help: charismatic, democratic, goals, mission, effectiveness, success, training.

➡ VIEWING

1. Rugby and the afternoon tea.
2. They talk about leadership.
3. He found inspiration in a poem.
4. He used a song. They listened to the words together.
5. The African anthem – *Nkosi sikelef' iAfrika* (*God bless Africa*).

(01:12:00-01:15:00) ➡ VIEWING

1. Open answer. It's a team game, similar to American soccer.
2. The South African team – the Springbokes.

(01:16:00-01:21:00) ➡ VIEWING

(3) I thank whatever gods may be
(6) I have not winced nor cried aloud
(9) Beyond this place of wrath and tears
(13) It matters not how strait the gate
(10) Looms but the horror of the shade
(5) In the fell clutch of circumstance
(12) Finds and shall find, me unafraid
(1) Out of the night that covers me
(8) My head is bloody, but unbowed.
(15) I am the master of my fate:
(2) Black as the pit from pole to pole
(16) I am the captain of my soul.
(4) For my unconquerable soul
(7) Under the bludgeoning of fate
(11) And yet the menace of the years
(14) How charged with punishment the scroll

➡ AFTER VIEWING

Open answer.

Bibliografia

ARTHUR, P. Why use video? A teacher's perspective, VSELT 2:4 (1999): 4.

CANNING, C. Visual support and language teaching, TESOL Arabia News, Volume 5:4, (1998): 3-4.

ELLIS, Rod. *The Study of Second Language Acquisition*. Oxford University Press, 1994.

GARDNER, Howard. *Frames of Mind – The Theory of Multiple Intelligences*. Harper Collins Publishers, 1993.

LONERGAN, Jack. *Video in Language teaching*. Cambridge: Cambridge University Press, 1984.

MCGOVERN, John (ed.). *Video applications in English Language teaching*. Oxford: Pergamon Press and the British Council, 1983.

NUNAN, David. *Designing Tasks for the Communicative Classroom*. Cambridge: Cambridge University Press, 1992.

SAVIGNON, Sandra. *Communicative Competence: Theory and Classroom Practice*. McGraw Hill, 1997.

SHERMAN, Jane. *Using Authentic Video in the Language Classroom*. Cambridge: Cambridge University Press, 2003.

TOMALIN, Barry. *Video, TV & Radio in the English Class*. London: Macmillan Publishers Ltd., 1986.

Sites da internet acessados

http://bogglesworldesl.com/lessons/MovieLesson.htm

www.nclrc.org/essentials/motivating/acquisition.htm

www.tefl.net/esl-articles/motivation-esl.htm

http://online.wsj.com/article/SB100014240527487034673045753831315927 67868.html

www.ru.nl/cls/research_0/communicative/more_information/communicative/